Preaching Like the Prophets

Preaching Like the Prophets

The Hebrew Prophets as Examples for the Practice of Pastoral Preaching

ROBERT A. CARLSON

WIPF & STOCK · Eugene, Oregon

PREACHING LIKE THE PROPHETS
The Hebrew Prophets as Examples for the Practice of Pastoral Preaching

Copyright © 2017 Robert A. Carlson. All rights reserved. Except for brief quotations in critical publications or reviews, no part of this book may be reproduced in any manner without prior written permission from the publisher. Write: Permissions, Wipf and Stock Publishers, 199 W. 8th Ave., Suite 3, Eugene, OR 97401.

Wipf & Stock
An Imprint of Wipf and Stock Publishers
199 W. 8th Ave., Suite 3
Eugene, OR 97401

www.wipfandstock.com

PAPERBACK ISBN: 978-1-5326-1334-0
HARDCOVER ISBN: 978-1-5326-1336-4
EBOOK ISBN: 978-1-5326-1335-7

Manufactured in the U.S.A.   FEBRUARY 7, 2017

Unless otherwise indicated, all scripture quotations are from the ESV® Bible (The Holy Bible, English Standard Version®), copyright © 2001 by Crossway, a publishing ministry of Good News Publishers. Used by permission. All rights reserved.

Scripture quotations designated (NASB) are taken from the New American Standard Bible® (NASB), copyright © 1960, 1962, 1963, 1968, 1971, 1972, 1973,1975, 1977, 1995 by The Lockman Foundation. Used by permission. www.Lockman.org.

Scripture quotations designated (NET) are from the NET Bible® copyright ©1996–2016 by Biblical Studies Press, L.L.C. http://netbible.org All rights reserved.

"To him who loves us and has freed us from our sins by his own blood" and "who has made us competent to be ministers of a new covenant."
(Rev 1:6; 2 Cor 3:6)

Contents

Acknowledgments | ix

    1   Hear the Prophets Preach | 1

Part One

    2   The Essential Prophet: "Thus Says the Lord . . ." | 13

    3   The Testimony of Jesus is the Spirit of Prophecy | 24

    4   The Spirit of the Lord is Upon Me . . . | 40

Part Two

    5   Opening Words and Opening Ears | 59

    6   A Word Fitly Spoken | 70

    7   Let Me Be Clear | 92

    8   Up Close and Personal | 110

    9   Show and Tell | 127

    10   Continuing to Preach like the Prophets | 140

Epilogue | 151
Bibliography | 153
Scripture Index | 161

Acknowledgments

Thank you to Julie who has been my constant help and encouragement through each phase of ministry, as well as throughout this project, which was initially birthed in our family devotions in the Minor Prophets. I am also thankful to our daughters Rebecca McCall and Ruth Zvinoera for their assistance in review and editing. Any remaining errors or awkwardness in the manuscript are mine, not theirs, but without their help my errors would be greatly multiplied.

This work would not have been possible without the preceding studies of the many outstanding scholars whose work I have referenced. More particularly, Robert Chisholm provided many helpful refinements and recommended several illuminating sources. Roger Raymer helped me to clarify certain points and was an encouragement throughout the project. Donald Sunukjian's personal instruction and writings have added significant clarity and relevance to my preaching and this work. Arturo Azurdia and Robert Smith each encouraged me in the Spirit's empowering in preaching and in completing this work in a form which would be of greater benefit to other preachers.

Finally, I am indebted to the elders and the members of Brush Prairie Baptist Church in Vancouver, Washington. I began these studies so that I might more faithfully and effectively preach the word of God to this wonderful church family. They have graciously nurtured my growth as a preaching pastor, and they have heard (and perhaps endured) many messages from the sermons of the Hebrew prophets during this project.

1

Hear the Prophets Preach

> But if all prophesy, and an unbeliever or outsider enters, he is convicted by all, he is called to account by all, the secrets of his heart are disclosed, and so, falling on his face, he will worship God and declare that God is really among you.
>
> 1 CORINTHIANS 14:24–25

As a preacher, the apostle Paul's words to the Corinthians haunt me. I want them to be true when I preach. I want them to be true in our church. When those who do not know Christ visit us, I want the word of God to come so near that it's as if the preacher knows them, that I somehow know what they are thinking. I want what I say as I preach to be so aimed at their heart, that it must be God. I want them to hear God himself imploring them through my message. I want them to tell others they heard from God here, and although it was both assuring and unsettling, they have to come back—regardless of the style of the music!

I want believers to have this experience as well. I want those who come hungry and expectant of a word from God, to hear it. I want them to feel the press of Nathan's finger on David's chest. I do not want it to be for that same terrible reason as David's guilt, although there will be times when it is. But I want God to speak so clearly through his messenger that it seems that I must have read their email or text messages. I want it to feel like the sermon has singled them out, so they cannot escape God's powerful and transforming message. I want them to know unmistakably that today, through the preacher, God spoke his word to them. I want my congregation to experience the truth of Calvin's words, "that if we come to church we shall not only hear a mortal man speaking but we shall feel (even by his secret power) that God is speaking to our souls."[1]

On any given Sunday a portion of the congregation will come to church discouraged. Life has been hard and their burden is heavy; the pressures threaten to overwhelm. They need to hear again from God through the preacher. They need to be reminded that God knows their hardship and his grace is sufficient. They need to see again the glory that is set before them as God himself would describe it to them, so that for the joy set before them they can endure their present cross. They need to hear the Spirit tell of the glory he is working in them through all of the stuff they may presently be enduring.

People coming to church desperately need to hear from God, not just hear from a preacher. I wish that this were their experience more often than it is. I cannot do what only God can do, but am I the messenger that I need to be? Or, have I let preaching become something less than it is supposed to be? How can I know what faithful pastoral preaching looks like? In 1 Corinthians 14:24–25 the apostle suggests that this dynamic experience of God's word ought to be the normal experience of the church gathered when the word of God is prophetically proclaimed. Normal that is, except for that awkward bit about prophesying.

It is not my purpose in this book to dive into the debate about the exact definition and nature of New Testament prophecy. That is an important topic, but it has already been written on extensively.[2] Instead, I will focus on the continuities and discontinuities between Old Testament prophets and New Testament preachers. There are clear parallels, as well as distinctions, between the Old Testament writing prophets and present era preaching pastors.

I will not attempt to prove that preachers are prophets. Rather, I will focus on the fact that the prophets were preachers. This is an important distinction. If we were to assert that preaching pastors are prophets, that would raise many issues for pastoral ministry including the inerrancy of preachers and the role of prediction in preaching. Greg's Scharf's recent clarification is helpful:

1. Calvin, *Ephesians*, 42.
2. See Grudem, *The Gift of Prophecy*; Thomas, "Prophecy Rediscovered," and Farnell, "Is the Gift of Prophecy for Today."

In the sub-apostolic New Testament era, preachers claim neither the sort of inspiration the Old Testament prophets had nor the authority of an eyewitness on a par with the apostles and therefore, their words from God for the good of the church are to be tested by apostolic doctrine already received (1 Cor 14:36–40; 1 Thess. 5:20–21). This does not mean that such words lack authority (Titus 2:15), only that the authority derives not from the fact that those words come *immediately* from God—for they do not—but from the fact that they come from God through the writings of the prophets and apostles (Acts 2:42; Eph 3:20). What prophets, apostles, and pastor-teachers have in common is that they speak for God, in his name, and on his behalf.[3]

However, focusing on the fact that the Old Testament prophets were essentially preachers opens the way to benefit from any parallels which exist between the preaching prophets and preaching pastors. This book will explore some of those salient parallels between prophets and preachers because I am convinced that the Hebrew prophets of the Old Testament are an under-utilized, yet profitable paradigm for pastoral preaching,

The prophets are important examples because there are not very many examples of pastoral preaching in the New Testament. Aside from Jesus's discourses,[4] there are few examples of a man called by God, preaching to those who are God's people and applying God's revelation to their lives. There are several examples of evangelistic preaching in the book of Acts. However, other than perhaps the book of Hebrews, most of the New Testament is composed of written epistles rather than oral preaching.[5]

On the other hand, the Old Testament prophets are rich with preaching prose. They are a treasure of neglected examples of spirit-inspired preaching.[6] This is not to suggest the study of the prophets' preaching has

---

3. Scharf and Chapell, *Let the Earth Hear His Voice*, 3.

4. Jesus preaches as the prophet par excellence, speaking God's word to a people under God's covenant, as the prophet which Moses promised (Deut 18:15–18). Therefore, Jesus discourses will also be a profitable example for pastoral preaching, if the sermons of the prophets who preceded him can be so considered.

5. Edwards, *A History of Preaching*, 6–7. Admittedly, Peter's and James's epistles, while clearly addressed as letters to a dispersed audience, are written by experienced preachers and have a strong oral component. When read in the church to their recipients, they would sound more sermonic than most of the Pauline epistles.

6. An example of this neglect by oversight is Quicke, "History of Preaching," 64–69. Quicke traces the history of preaching from the New Testament era to the present, showing a break from the synagogue style of explaining a reading to herald preaching, yet he gives no mention of the prophets as predecessors of herald preaching. This does not

been completely neglected. In fact, the following chapters will rely on a considerable body of rhetorical analysis of the prophets. However, the main thrust of current rhetorical analysis has focused on understanding the message and purpose of the prophets, rather than applying the prophets' rhetoric to pastoral preaching. This is the gap which this book explores: parallels which exist between the preaching of the prophets and the preaching of pastors.

The prophets were men of God; some were called to preach in a place far from their own home and some where called to preach to people they had lived among all their lives. In either case, they preached to those whom God had chosen to be his unique people, from among all the nations of the earth. Under the divine supervision of the Spirit of God these preachers apply the word of God given hundreds of years earlier through Moses to the present circumstances in which God's people now live. They remind people of what God has done for them. They confront sin that is contrary to God's revealed word and urge God's people to walk in God's ways in light of his mercy toward them and their standing as his chosen people. They give hope as they speak of what God had promised he would do, even though the people had not yet seen that promise fulfilled and needed to live toward it by faith. Most of all, they continually point to Christ and his coming.

"Called to preach . . . applying the word of God . . . recalling God's promised future . . ."—am I describing the prophets preaching to Israel or pastors preaching to the church? As you can see, the essence of what the Old Testament prophets were doing in their era has much in common with the essence of pastoral preaching today.

The New Testament provides another example of the parallels between Old Testament prophets and pastoral preachers. That example is the book of Hebrews. Many expositors have suggested that the book of Hebrews was originally written as a sermon to be preached.[7] It is clearly written to an audience in the church era, under the New Covenant; however, it has a definite Old Testament resonance. The author (or preacher) reminds them from the Law of Moses of what God has done for them. He reminds them of who they are as God's people and gives several prophetic warnings. In technique similar to the prophets, Hebrews uses the assurance of God's

---

suggest that Quicke would not consider the prophets as an earlier example of a preaching herald. But, it does illustrate the tendency to begin thinking of the history of preaching as parallel to the history of the church. In refreshing contrast, Larsen, *The Company of the Preachers*, 26–30, agrees with Broadus that "the prophets were preachers."

7. Lane, *Hebrews 1–8*, lxix–lxxiv.

redemptive work in the past and the hope of a glorious future to exhort God's people to live faithfully during a present difficult time of opposition and hardships. Most importantly, the message continually focuses on Jesus as the fullness of God's previous promises. The book of Hebrews has the tone and timbre of an Old Testament prophet, but is clearly a sermon preached to the church, proclaiming the risen Christ.

The same general elements of content can also be found in the apostles' New Testament epistles. They build on previous special revelation, often quoting the Old Testament. The epistles remind God's people who they are in Christ and therefore how they should live in light of their redemption. The gospel of Jesus is, to the authors of the epistles, what the redemptive exodus event was to the writing prophets. The epistles not only look back; they, like the prophets, look forward. They bring light to the present by remembering and anticipating. They call us to remember what God has done and confidently hope in what God has promised. The word of God through both Old Testament prophets and New Testament apostles calls God's people to live as God's people ought to live between the two horizons of what God has done redemptively and what he will do eschatologically.

However, there are two significant differences between the epistles and the prophets. The first difference is one of form: the epistles are written as letters, not sermons. This does not ignore the fact that they are letters written to be read in the churches. In fact some of the epistles sound sermonic, such as the letters of Peter and James.[8] However, in the epistles the sermon has been adapted into a literary form. The prophets, on the other hand, are comprised largely of oral sermons framed with biographical narrative.

The second difference between the epistles and the prophets is more significant: they each speak to different contexts in different historical eras. The apostles and the church fathers who followed them preached in a very different context from that of many preaching pastors today. In the first century, the message of the gospel was strange and different; this radical preaching of a resurrected savior had not been heard before. Today, many pastors preach among a society which has heard of the gospel, or at least a caricature of it, and moved on to something else. Our message is not radically new; it is perceived by many who hear us to be out of date and past its prime. Os Guinness puts it well:

---

8. See Kistemaker, *Exposition of the Epistle of James and the Epistles of John*, 2–4, and *Exposition of Peter and Jude*, 22.

> For the early Christian apologists in the time of the Roman Empire, the challenge was to introduce a message so novel that it was strange to its first hearers, and then to set out what the message meant for the classical age and its sophisticated and assured ways of thinking. For much of the advanced modern world today, in contrast, the challenge is to restate something so familiar that people know it so well that they do not know it, yet at the same time are convinced that they are tired of it.[9]

Like preachers today, the prophets also preached to a generation that was familiar with Israel's covenant with Yahweh as a religious heritage from which they had since progressed or outgrown. Their audience might have opined: "This talk of Yahweh is so 1400s, does anyone still believe that stuff?" Gary Smith describes the societal context during the ministries of Zephaniah and Jeremiah:

> Some pagan prophets and priests carried out their roles in ways that profaned God's sacred laws. The process of secularization caused others to ignore God rather than trust Him. Some concluded that God was unimportant, for the plausibility structures that supported the ancient Mosaic worldview were undermined by the pluralistic tendencies of Manasseh.[10]

During the era of the prophets Israel retained many of the trappings of a shared civil religion which was similar to Paul's description of the later days, "having an appearance of godliness but denying its power" (2 Tim 3:5). Walter Brueggemann finds similarities between the societal crisis in contemporary western culture and that of ancient Jerusalem. He describes the prophet's ministry as confronting an ideology of exceptionalism which distorted the current spiritual reality and fostered unrealistic notions of entitlement, privilege and superiority.[11] In this sense, the context in which we

---

9. Guinness, *Fool's Talk*, 28.

10. Smith, *The Prophets As Preachers*, 169.

11. Brueggemann, *Reality, Grief, Hope: Three Urgent Prophetic Tasks*, 33–34. Brueggemann summarizes: "In imagining its own ultimacy, the Jerusalem establishment had shelved the ultimacy of the God who will not be mocked and consequently had failed to recognize its own penultimacy, its dependence upon and accountability to YHWH." While Brueggemann applies his comparison to American society as a whole, the comparison is especially relevant between the Old Testament covenant nation and American evangelicals who put confidence in a manifest destiny as a "Christian nation." Grieving the loss of that Christian nation, they put their hope in the revival of an American Christian nation rather than in God's new reality, which the prophets pointed toward then and preaching pastors must redirect hope to today.

preach is more similar to the days of the prophets then it is to the first century. Thus, the earlier examples of the preaching of the prophets is possibly even more important to preachers today than the New Testament examples of preaching which are historically and theologically closer to us. While the epistles and the gospels contain our message, now more than ever, the prophets should inform our method.

This returns us to the central question: can the Old Testament prophets serve as a biblical model for pastoral preaching? Should pastors preach prophetically? Perhaps it depends on what we mean by preaching prophetically. Does this mean that people should fill in the blank pages in the back of their Bibles with the words of their prophetic pastor? Should we add to our Bibles "The Gospel of John Piper"? There are many faulty notions about prophetic preaching, so it is important to first define what we mean by prophetic preaching, or preaching like the prophets.

It might be helpful to borrow terminology used in other discussions concerning the relationship between the Old Testament and the New Testament by speaking of the continuities and discontinuities between prophets and preachers. I am probably not alone in anticipating that there are continuities, and yet preachers who have blushed at Isaiah's and Micah's extreme object lessons (Isa 20:3; Mic 1:8) also hope that I will establish some amount of discontinuity between the prophet's practice and our own.

I do not suggest that the prophetic books are intended as handbooks on preaching. Rather, I agree with Bryan Chapell that, "Though the Bible is not intended to be a homiletics textbook, it indicates valuable tools for communication that we should consider valuable for preaching."[12] There is nothing in the prophets to suggest that their purpose in writing was to provide a manual for effective oral rhetoric. I will focus on the preaching of the prophets as descriptive, rather than prescriptive. For example, when pastors have the opportunity to hear the sermon from a highly gifted and seasoned preacher, we benefit from both their exhortation and their example. We learn not only from what they say, but how they say it. We are blessed by the word of God through them and also blessed to learn something about the art of effective preaching from them.

Similarly, preaching pastors can find the prophets to be profitable examples of men of God who have gone before us as preachers of the word of God. In reading and studying the prophets, preachers can benefit not only from their message, but also their method. We can benefit from their

---

12. Chapell, *Christ-Centered Preaching*, 187.

doctrine and their delivery, just as a homiletic student reviewing the work of a seasoned preacher can benefit from both the exhortation and the example of his sermon.

Considering the Old Testament prophets as a pattern for pastoral preaching also begs the question, "Which prophet is preaching?" Are the books of the prophets really composed of the words of the prophets? In this work I am setting aside issues of authorship and redaction in order to focus on rhetoric in its more classic sense as the art of persuasion. Others, too, have already called for increased attention to rhetoric as persuasion in the Old Testament. For example, David Howard states that the foundational aspect of rhetoric as a means of persuasion "has been all but lacking in Old Testament rhetorical criticism" studies.[13] Reed Lessing urges renewed study of the orality of written Old Testament texts so that "we may learn from the prophet's homiletical moves, structures, and strategies."[14]

I am assuming, a priori, a more conservative evangelical stance concerning the authorship and dating of the writing prophets. I am taking the books as they are presented in the canon, as the poetry and prose of the prophets whose names they bear.[15] I suspect it is more likely that someone holding this view would attempt a project which suggests that these historical prophets, from a particular historical context, can be useful examples to us who preach today. However, even scholars who believe the prophetic books to be heavily redacted and containing only remnants of the original oral messages can still agree that the canonical form of each of the prophetic books are presented as if they were the record of a single prophet's preaching. Thus one's view of authorship and redaction is not critical to using the prophets as a biblical model of pastoral preaching.

The following chapters are divided into two parts. In chapters 2–4 I will consider the ministry, message, and means of the prophets. In these chapters I will clarify what I mean by prophetic preaching, or preaching like the prophets. Next, I will discuss the essential message of the prophets and continuities which exist between the essential message of prophets and preachers. Then I will demonstrate the continuity of the means God

13. Howard, "Rhetorical Criticism in Old Testament Studies," 88.

14. Lessing, "Orality in the Prophets," 153.

15. Clendenen, "Textlinguistics and Prophecy," 398–99, agrees: "my working hypothesis is that each book came directly or indirectly from the prophet and was produced with a coherent structure. Whether or not there were later additions to the books is impossible to prove, but it is hermeneutically advisable to assume that the books were produced in the form that has been transmitted to us."

has ordained for the effectual proclaiming of his message, whether by the prophets, apostles, or present-day preaching pastors.

Having established significant continuity between prophets and pastors in their ministry, message and means, chapters 5–10 will focus on the method of the prophets. In these chapters we will look more closely at how the prophets preached, comparing current rhetorical analysis of the prophets to techniques which are considered by current homiletics texts to be essentials in the practice of effective preaching. I will survey recent work in rhetorical analysis of the prophets, which will demonstrate that there was considerable and studied intentionality in their preaching. Recently, the major application of rhetorical analysis has been to interpreting the prophets,[16] but pastoral preachers can take that benefit one step further by also applying these rhetorical studies to better understand how the prophets communicated as masterful, divinely-inspired preachers of God's word.

This work is not intended to be an exhaustive analysis of the preaching technique of the prophets. It is intended to be an encouragement for preaching pastors to read the prophets from a new perspective: as a fellow preacher learning from inspired veterans. The goal of this work is to identify the essential ministry, message, means, and rhetorical methods of the prophets, and discuss how these same essentials can and should strengthen a pastor's prophetic preaching today. It is my hope that you will not only recognize that the prophets can be a model for pastoral preaching, but that you will also become convinced that the preaching prophets are examples that we must refer to for powerful and persuasive preaching today. The one thing I hope you gain from this work is that preachers can and must learn from the prophets' work.

---

16. For example, see Lessing, "Preaching Like the Prophets" and Chisholm, "Structure, Style, and the Prophetic Message."

PART ONE

Part One

2

The Essential Prophet: "Thus Says the Lord..."

To be a prophet is both a distinction and an affliction.

ABRAHAM HESCHEL[1]

Throughout the church era there have been recurring calls for prophetic preaching,[2] but this call has meant different things to different authors. For some it has meant bold, fearless preaching of the word of God,[3] a particular preaching style. Others have suggested a functional definition: for the sixteenth-century reformer William Perkins, "Preaching the word is prophesying."[4] Some have boldly equated prophetic and pastoral ministry, while others draw a stark distinction between the two.

Conservatives have often limited prophetic preaching to the prophets and the specific special revelation they were given concerning future events. They may see the excesses of contemporary predictive preaching as reason to minimize the prophets as an appropriate model for pastoral

---

1. Heschel, *The Prophets*, 1:17–18

2. For example, see Spalding, "The Hebrew Prophet and the Christian Preacher"; Shelp and Sunderland, *The Pastor as Prophet*; Devor, "Whatever Happened to Prophetic Preaching?"; Willimon, "Would That All the Lord's People Were Prophets"; Sensing, "A Call to Prophetic Preaching," and Lessing, "Preaching Like the Prophets."

3. Ayer, "Pulpit Prophet," 291–93.

4. Perkins, *The Art of Prophesying with the Calling of the Ministry*, Kindle location 98.

preaching. Pentecostals and others have identified prophetic preaching with a propensity for immediate inspiration and ecstatic utterance that assumes unquestioned authority. As one Pentecostal author states, "the Pentecostal preacher is prone to say, 'the Lord spoke to me,' or 'the Spirit said,' thus claiming divine authorization or legitimization for one's message and leadership."[5] Such unqualified confidence in the inerrancy of the preacher can easily lead to abuse. Finally, many recent calls for prophetic preaching refer to an emphasis on ethics and equality, especially as they relate to social justice issues. Resisting this trend, Willimon suggests, "The notion of prophets as irascible, lone, carping social critics, while congenial to our radically individualized culture, has little to do with prophecy in Israel or in the church."[6]

In this cacophony of connotations surrounding prophetic preaching, it is no wonder that many disregard any continuity between the Old Testament prophets and Christian pastoral preaching. However, in sharply distinguishing prophets from preachers, we are overlooking one of the richest biblical examples we have for the ministry of preaching God's word. As stated previously, we do not need to believe that preachers are prophets in order to recognize that the prophets were preachers. This distinction sets aside the troublesome issues that come with equating pastors to prophets, such as infallibility and predictive authority while focusing on the practice of preaching that both prophets and pastors share.

In the next few pages, we will roll up our sleeves and do a little lexical and exegetical work defining the basic meaning of the term "prophet" and the essential nature of the prophetic task. This will help to clarify how to answer the contemporary calls for prophetic preaching in a way which most closely aligns with Scripture.

A BIBLICAL DEFINITION OF THE OLD TESTAMENT PROPHET

Defining the essence of the prophet's ministry should begin with the meaning of the word "prophet." "Prophet" is derived from the Greek word προφήτης, *prophetēs*, which was used in the Septuagint, the Greek translation of the Old Testament, to translate the Hebrew noun נביא, *nabi*. The noun *nabi*, which is regularly used to refer to the Old Testament Hebrew prophets, most simply

---

5. Leoh, "A Pentecostal Preacher as an Empowered Witness," 53.
6. Willimon, "Would That All the Lord's People Were Prophets," 17.

means "spokesman, speaker or prophet"[7] or "a speaker, herald, preacher" and "one who has been called.["8] According to the *Theological Wordbook of the Old Testament*, "The essential in the word is that of authorized spokesman" and the movement of scholars "has been away from regarding the active idea of speaking ecstatically as the essential meaning of prophesying."[9] This explains why the Septuagint translated *nabi* with *prophetēs*, which according to Liddell and Scott, refers to "one who speaks for God and interprets his will to man."[10] Similarly, Danker and Bauer define *prophetēs* as a "proclaimer and interpreter of the divine revelation."[11] Martti Nissinen concludes that a prophet is "a person sent by God to teach the people and give them messages from God" and prophecy denotes "primarily the activity of transmitting and interpreting the divine will."[12]

In a prophet's ministry, foretelling is secondary to forth-telling as Nissinen states: "if intermediation is seen as the primary quality of prophecy, the eventual predictive aspect is subordinate to this quality."[13] This is not to say that the predictive element of a prophet's ministry was incidental or unimportant. C. Hassell Bullock balances these points:

> Although it can accurately be said that the prophets were basically preachers—that is, that they spoke to their own times and situations, interpreting current events of history in light of God's will for Israel—the predictive element was a distinctive part of their message (Amos 3:7). Subtract that and, as Alfred Guillaume has said, they would become preachers and not prophets.[14]

7. BDB, 611 s.v. נביא. See also *TWOT*, 2:544–45.
8. Koehler, et al, *Hebrew and Aramaic Lexicon*, 661.
9. *TWOT*, 2:544.
10. LSJ, 704.
11. BDAG, 723.
12. Nissinen, "What is Prophecy?" 19–20. See also Bullock, *Old Testament Prophetic Books*, 15–17. Bullock points to positive Akkadian roots for נביא that mean either "to speak" or "to call." These roots underscore the main characteristic of a prophet as one who speaks for God or one who is called by God (to speak for him), rather than one who predicts the future. The prophets only predicted future events when that was part of the message God called them to speak.
13. Nissinen, 23. See also Spalding, "The Hebrew Prophet and the Christian Preacher," 285. Spalding observes that "the great service to which the predictive element in prophecy has been put in Christian apologetics during the past two centuries has largely obscured the broader and more fundamental idea which really more fully possesses it, as a revelation of the Divine Will."
14. Bullock, *Old Testament Prophetic Books*, 16–17.

Part One

Bullock here implies that the prophets are more than preachers. Or, putting it logically, the prophets are a subset or special class of preachers. Therefore, while we must not assume that preachers are prophets, we can assume that the prophets were preachers.

It is clear that the Hebrew and Greek words used to refer to the Old Testament writing prophets in the Old Testament emphasize that the primary aspect of a prophet's role was forth-telling as God's spokesman. Thus the prophets were essentially God's messengers, and the message they were given to declare included foretelling future events.

Alongside the lexical evidence, another important factor in arriving at a biblical definition of the prophet's ministry is to consider how the Bible itself defines or at least provides a definitive connotation for the term prophet. One of the first uses of the Hebrew word *nabi* (prophet) occurs in Exodus 7:1–2. Here, in response to Moses's complaint that he cannot speak to Pharaoh, the Lord designates Aaron as Moses's "prophet" and declares that Moses shall speak all that God commands him to Aaron, and then Aaron shall tell Pharaoh. Aaron, as the "prophet" of Moses, is Moses's divinely appointed spokesperson.[15]

The prophet's role as spokesperson is evident in the hallmark phrase in the preaching of the prophets: "Thus says the Lord." This phrase, or the similar "The word of the Lord came to . . ." occurs in nearly all of the writing prophets.[16] "Thus says the Lord" introduces oracles which remind of God's past work, confront present realities or predict the future, but what is clear, regardless of the temporal aspect, is that the word spoken is from the Lord and is spoken on his behalf.

Similarly, one of the foundational texts anticipating future prophetic ministry presents the prophet as one who is raised up by God, who will speak publically for God in the assembly and must be listened to, because he speaks God's words in God's name (Deut 18:15–22). The writings of Moses also required that later prophets who would arise must speak in harmony with what God had previously said in the Torah, the five books of Moses. Deuteronomy 13:1–5 warns against a prophet who says "let us go after

15. *TWOT*, 544–45 has a very helpful discussion of the definitive uses of נביא in the Old Testament.

16. The only exceptions are Daniel, which is narrative in style rather than hortatory, and Lamentations, which is a pastoral lament traditionally attributed to Jeremiah who uses "Thus says the Lord" and "declares the Lord" more often than any of the other prophets. Even the narrative of Jonah identifies Jonah's basic function as a prophet to be one sent by God to deliver God's message (Jonah 1:1–2).

other gods" or leads the people to "leave the way in which the Lord your God commanded you to walk" (through Moses). Such a prophet should not be followed or feared, even if things he predicted come to pass. Any predictive aspect of the prophet's ministry was subordinate to his fidelity to God's covenant with his people, as proscribed in the Torah. Clendenen has ably demonstrated from 2 Kings 17:13 that the prophets must be understood as "messengers of God" who functioned as "covenant mediators" or covenant "enforcers."[17] Similarly, D. Stuart has demonstrated that the Old Testament prophets were dependent on and accountable to Moses and the Torah for their preaching:

> The evidence supports the conclusion that the OT prophets carried on their inspired ministries within a tradition that consciously and directly went back to the ancient Mosaic covenant as expressed in the Pentateuch, i.e., its first statement in Exodus-Leviticus-Numbers and its renewal in Deuteronomy. The prophets had not the slightest sense that they were creating any new doctrine but considered themselves spokespersons for Yahweh, who through them called his people back to obedience to the covenant he had given them many centuries before, and reminded them of its curses and blessings, which Yahweh had sworn to honor.
>
> Nearly all of the content of the classical (writing) prophets' oracles revolve around the announcement of the near-time fulfillment of covenantal curses and the end-time fulfillment of covenantal restoration blessings. They speak of little else than these two topics: how and why God's people may expect to be punished by a variety of disasters soon, and how and why they may expect to be rescued and restored eventually.[18]

Likewise, Gary Smith describes the prophets' application of the Torah to later generations:

> The prophets communicated principles that were known from earlier traditions in the Torah or earlier prophets to legitimate what they said. They also gave imaginative new externalizations that ran counter to the cultural worldview of their audiences. Their teachings were often based on past revelation in the law, but

---

17. Clendenen, "Textlinguistics and Prophecy," 386. Also see Merrill, *Deuteronomy*, 273. In his discussion of Deut 18:16–17, Merrill describes the prophets as "covenant enforcers" after Moses.

18. Stuart, *Hosea-Jonah*, xxxii. See also Long, "Prophetic Preaching." 385–59. Long concludes that the prophetic is not innovation which opposes the tradition of faith, but rather it opposes a contemporary departure from the tradition.

they were not limited by ideas formulated to apply to people in an earlier cultural context.[19]

Thus the prophets' messages are founded on Torah and in harmony with it, although they did not merely repeat or restate Moses to a later generation. God increasingly revealed himself in the progressive revelation of the prophets, and yet their messages are rooted in Moses. Even the prophets' predictions of coming judgment and future restoration are not new, but are also dependent on and in agreement with the previous revelation given through Moses in Deuteronomy 28.[20] Therefore, the prophets "should not be seen only as radical innovators or rebels against the laws and traditions. They recalled tradition to the people, showing them how God had acted in the past, and what the covenant had taught, and insisting that Israel not forget."[21] In reality, the prophets were not social progressives, but were conserving the traditions and revelations of the past. As Sensing writes:

> They were concerned with reformation not innovation, confrontation not creation, revival not change. Therefore, preservation of the tradition was central as they reapplied the covenant to new situations, re-envisioned the present in light of the past in order to insure future fidelity.[22]

To summarize, the key elements of our definition are first, the Old Testament prophet was primarily God's spokesman, one who speaks for God based on God's previously given special revelation, whether reminding of the past, confronting the present or declaring what will come in the future. Second, prophetic fore-telling is secondary to forth-telling. Third, the Old Testament prophet's ministry of proclamation is primarily to a specific people who are in a covenant relationship to God, and the words of the prophet hold the audience accountable to that covenant. The prophet's message was not entirely innovative, but was accountable to the revelation previously given at the establishment of God's covenant with his people. The prophets applied the word God given by Moses, to a covenant people

---

19. Smith, *The Prophets As Preachers*, 341.

20. Understanding the foretelling of the prophets as dependent upon the covenantal curses and blessings and restoration promised by Moses (see especially Deut 28) is also a significant factor in the right interpretation of the prophet's predictions.

21. Boadt, *Reading the Old Testament*, 549. See also von Rad, *The Message of the Prophets*, 12. von Rad describes the prophets as being deeply rooted in the tradition of Moses and raising the alarm when Israel has strayed from it.

22. Sensing, "A Call to Prophetic Preaching," 148.

and their circumstances several hundred years removed from the original revelation.

THE ESSENTIAL PROPHET AND THE ESSENCE OF PREACHING

It is not difficult to see in these key elements the continuities between these preachers of Israel and preachers in the church. Preaching pastors are also called to speak authoritatively as a God-ordained spokesman based on his special revelation. The essence of our call is to "Preach the word" (2 Tim 4:2). We do not preach "a word" or "our word." We preach "the word," the Scripture which is "inspired by God and profitable for teaching, for reproof, for correction, for training in righteousness" (2 Tim 3:16 NASB). Donald Sunukjian captures the pastoral essence of this essential aspect of preaching, when he responds to the question, "How do you see yourself when you are up there preaching?"

> I see myself as standing with you, under the word of God saying, "Look what God is saying to us." . . .
>
> In my mind's eye, I saw myself as standing, not over the congregation, but among them, holding open a Bible, showing its pages to them, saying, "This is God's word—inspired, inerrant, authoritative. It tells us what we need to know—what to think, how to act, what's ahead. It gives us truth. Isn't it wonderful? It's what God is saying to us!"[23]

Graeme Goldsworthy notes that "the common conviction of evangelicals is that the Bible is the word of God and that we have a commission to proclaim it."[24] This is why we commit to expository preaching which has been defined by Haddon Robinson as "the communication of a biblical concept, derived from and transmitted through a historical, grammatical, and literary study of a passage in its context, which the Holy Spirit first applies to the personality and experience of the preacher, then through the preacher, applies to his hearers."[25]

Pastors preaching God's word share the authority which resides in God's word with the prophets who preached before us. Where the prophets

---

23. Sunukjian, *Biblical Preaching*, 9.
24. Goldsworthy, *Preaching the Whole Bible As Christian Scripture*, 32.
25. Robinson, *Biblical Preaching*, 21.

said, "Thus says the Lord," pastors say "Thus the Lord has said." Similarly, the pastor's preaching is also accountable to the written word of God previously given, just as the prophets were accountable to Moses. We are not limited to Moses, even as the prophets were given additional progressive revelation. But, everything revealed through them was in harmony with what was already given. Preachers today should not claim the same inspiration as the Hebrew prophets, but we should be inspired by the fuller revelation which has been entrusted to us. As John Koessler points out:

> Every preacher feels the weight of the prophetic mantle, when standing before the congregation. The preacher, however, differs from the prophet in an important respect. Although both aim to communicate the Word of God, the preacher's words are not God's words. When the prophet's spoke, they were 'carried along' by the Holy Spirit (2 Pet 1:21). Such language, while not necessarily implying dictation, speaks clearly of divine control. The prophets spoke from God. This unique ministry of the Holy Spirit guaranteed that the true prophet would only say what God intended. The expositor, on the other hand, speaks about God's Word.[26]

Koessler's qualification serves as a reminder of why it is critical for the preaching pastor to adhere devotedly to the intention of the text, the burden of the original, inspired author. A faithful preacher must "hold firm to the trustworthy word" (Tit 1:9). When we stand before God's church, we need to be able to clearly and convincingly tell them, "This is what God says."[27] This is the privilege we share with the prophets. Like the prophets, we might be innovative and creative in methods of communication, but we dare not innovate when it comes to the message. As the prophets were bound to Moses, we are bound by the theological tradition of "the faith that was once for all delivered to the saints" (Jude 3).

We not only have the word of God through Moses and the prophets, we also have the word of God through the Lord Jesus and his Apostles. The words we preach must always be accountable to that special revelation which has preceded us. If we drift from the word of God to our own word or opinion, we are no longer confessing or saying the same thing as God has already said. Then it will be as true for us as for any prophet of Israel who proclaimed a message that did not agree with what God had already

---

26. Koessler, "Losing the Center," 21.
27. Easley, "Why Expository Preaching," 36.

revealed, the people should not hear him or fear him (Deut 13:1–5). Zack Eswine has said it well to "preachers in a post-everything world":

> Prophetic preaching calls people back to covenant faithfulness. Prophets are preachers of memory. They remind of first love. They love the old truth and the God who spoke it. The Old Testament prophets are people of the book. They speak congruently with what has been written; they write what has been spoken. Those seeking a prophetic analogy imitate this approach.
>
> In contrast, the thieving preacher is a "word stealer." He makes up his own messages and speaks on his own authority. He offers prophetic forgeries to people because he speaks his own as if they were from God.[28]

Another continuity between the prophets and pastors is that both preach primarily or especially to God's covenant people. The prophets held Israel accountable to the words of the Law given through Moses. They preached with reference to God's special revelation given several hundred years earlier, and they applied that same covenant to the present situation among God's people. They spoke of ancient warnings which were still valid and ancient promises which were still to be fulfilled. Similarly, pastors preach from special revelation given several hundred years earlier, to God's people in their present situations. The task of pastors and prophets is similar, preaching across horizons: from the situation in which the word of God was originally given to the contemporary situation in which God's people live.[29] Both prophet and pastor preach the word of God across this historical gap to God's people who desperately and urgently need to hear from their God. Prophets spoke across that historical gap from previous revelation to their contemporary setting under the inspiration of the Holy Spirit, while pastors do so by the illumination of the Holy Spirit, but we will consider that distinction in a following chapter.

Someone might object that the prophets did not always seem to be preaching to God's covenant people Israel. Isaiah, Jeremiah, and Ezekiel all declare God's coming judgment on many nations (Isa 13–21; Jer 46–51; Ezek 25–32). Obadiah and Nahum preach oracles against Edom and Assyria. Semantically, these oracles are addressed to the nations, however, the

---

28. Eswine, *Preaching to a Post-Everything World*, 120.

29. For further discussions on bridging ancient and contemporary horizons in homiletics, see Robinson, *Biblical Preaching*, 73–75; Sunukjian, *Biblical Preaching*, 27–30; Lovell and Richardson, *Sustaining Preachers and Preaching*, 122; and Greidanus, *The Modern Preacher and the Ancient Text*, 137–39.

intended effect of these oracles is to remind Israel, the intended audience, of God's sovereignty over the nations. Isaiah, Jeremiah, and Ezekiel all insert their prophecies concerning the nations within their prophecies concerning Israel. Obadiah concludes his vision of Edom's fall, with a pronouncement of Israel's rescue and restoration.[30] Even Nahum can be understood to be giving those in Israel who suffer under Assyrian oppression a reminder of "their own majestic and omnipotent God" who will judge their ruthless oppressor.[31] Therefore, if we conclude that the prophets spoke primarily to or for the edification of those who were in a covenantal relationship to God, this suggests a greater continuity between the prophets and preaching pastors, than between the prophets and missionaries or evangelists. Just as evangelists and missionaries can benefit from the examples of Peter and Paul's preaching in the book of Acts, pastors who preach to God's church can benefit from listening in as the prophets preach to God's people Israel.

Still, like the prophets, our preaching also has implications for those outside the covenant community. At times pastoral preaching is overheard by those who visit among God's people. At other times we intentionally, evangelistically preach to those who are not in covenant relationship with God, while being overheard by the church. Just as Israel benefited from hearing prophetic words to the nations, so the church is edified by hearing the gospel, with its hope and promise, as it is preached evangelistically for the benefit of those who don't know Christ. Like the prophets, pastors will also be God's spokesman or messenger to the unsaved nations, concerning their accountability to God and their need for God's salvation. However, that message does not only benefit "the nations" or those outside of a covenant relationship with God. God's church is also edified by the reminder that judgment is coming on the rebellious nations. This will encourage the church in times of persecution and stir her evangelistic zeal in times of comfort and apathy. In this sense, the pastor as God's messenger is a catalyst for the church to also be messengers and ambassadors for God. In this way a "prophetic" pastor provokes the church to be a "prophetic community."[32]

Therefore, prophets and pastors are both God's messengers, God's spokesman, called to speak or proclaim God's word. We both speak God's

---

30. Clendenen, "Textlinguistics and Prophecy," 395–96. Clendenen describes the main message of the oracles of Obadiah and Nahum as a message of hope and call to repentance in light of that hope because "In judging his enemies God will deliver his people."

31. Feinberg, *The Minor Prophets*, 189.

32. Brueggemann, *The Prophetic Imagination*, 62.

word predominantly to God's people, prophets to Israel under the Old Covenant, pastors to the church of God under the New Covenant. The covenantal relationship of the prophets' audience to God is an important factor in understanding the prophets' message. This aspect has too often been underappreciated, leading to faulty generalizations about the nature of the prophets' message and thus the nature of prophetic preaching today.

Because pastors are "standing on the shoulders of the prophets"[33] in speaking God's word as God's messengers to God's people, we must give careful attention to the substance of our message. We are accountable to the revelation from God, from which we speak. Just as the prophets were accountable to God's previous revelation to Moses, pastors are accountable to God's previous revelation given to Moses, and the prophets, and the apostles and prophets of the New Testament. This accountability leads us to consider more fully the continuities in the message of the prophets and pastors which will be considered in the following chapter.

The Second Helvetic Confession states that, "The preaching of the word of God is the word of God." This does not mean that all preaching carries the same authority as the prophets. Helvetica does not assert that "preaching is the word of God," but rather that "the preaching of the word of God is the word of God." F. B. Meyer captures the reformation heritage of expository preaching and then links that heritage back to the grand privilege and responsibility which preaching pastors share with the prophets: "The reformers, the Puritans, the pastors of the Pilgrim fathers were essentially expositors. They did not announce their own particular opinions, which might be a matter of private interpretation or doubtful disposition, but taking their stand on scripture, drove home their message with irresistible effect with 'Thus saith the Lord.'"[34]

May we preach with the same prophetic confidence because we derive our preaching from the same source as the prophets: "Thus saith the Lord," for we too are his messengers.

---

33. Sandnes, *Paul, One of the Prophets*, 146.
34. Meyer, *Expository Preaching*, 60.

3

The Testimony of Jesus is the Spirit of Prophecy

Our society finds truth too strong a medicine to digest undiluted. In its purest form, truth is not a polite tap on the shoulder. It is a howling reproach. What Moses brought down from the Mount Sinai were not the Ten Suggestions; they are commandments.

TED KOPPEL[1]

If any one thing consistently points to the uniqueness and lasting greatness of the Hebrew prophets, it is their message.

JACK R. LUNDBOM[2]

The previous chapter offered a biblical definition of the essential ministry of the Old Testament prophet which informs a biblical understanding of prophetic preaching. Prophets, like preachers, are essentially messengers of the Lord. If preachers and prophets share the same calling as God's messengers, there should also be some continuity in the essential message of prophets and preachers. Someone might initially respond: "Wait, prophets and preachers are messengers in two different eras under two different covenants, the Sinai Covenant of Moses and the New Covenant inaugurated by Christ in his death. Surely we have different messages." It is true that

1. Shelly, *Written in Stone*, 10.
2. Lundbom, *The Hebrew Prophets*, 8.

our messages must be different in certain ways. Progressive revelation requires it. Yet, in some foundational ways, this chapter will demonstrate an essential continuity between the message of the prophets and the message of preachers.

To put it plainly, if we as pastors want to learn from the preaching of the prophets, we should consider, "What did the prophets preach?" Or, perhaps more nuanced, "What continuities should we expect between the message preached by the prophets and the message preached by pastors today?" In this chapter we will confront a common misconception concerning the content of prophetic preaching, and then suggest two essential elements of genuine prophetic preaching which are too often overlooked.

IS PROPHETIC PREACHING SOCIAL JUSTICE PREACHING?

Recognizing that many of the oracles of the writing prophets concerned matters of unrighteousness and injustice has led many current authors to call for "prophetic preaching" that addresses social issues and matters of economic and political injustice.[3] Prophetic preaching is understood to refer to "speaking truth to power." Furthermore, some authors in this school of thought understand their social justice version of prophetic preaching to be largely incompatible with pastoral preaching. Stanley Hauerwas provides an example of this view:

> Being a pastor and being a prophet are roles most assume cannot be easily reconciled. Indeed, many claim you cannot be both. Some pastors, such as Martin Luther King Jr., may be prophetic, but most pastors have to carry on the day-to-day tasks of ministry that are anything but prophetic... the moral outrage that fuels the fires of a prophetic calling seems incompatible with the kind of openness necessary to being a caring pastor....[4]

Hauerwas continues by discussing how Amos refers to Israel as fattened "cows of Bashan" and unrelentingly condemns the self-indulgent lives they have lived oppressing the poor. He concludes that the prophet Amos could hardly be called Pastor Amos:

---

3. Tisdale, *Prophetic Preaching*, offers several different definitions of prophetic preaching in the social criticism stream. See also McMickle, *Where Have All the Prophets Gone* and Park, "Speaking of Hope: Prophetic Preaching."

4. Hauerwas, "The Pastor as Prophet," 27.

> This kind of prophetic role simply does not seem compatible with the best insights of clinical pastoral education methodology. These "cows" are also people in pain who deserve the same kind of care that he thinks should be directed toward the poor. If we are to minister to the "cows of Bashan," it seems that Amos's rhetoric, as well as his practice, will have to change.[5]

This over-emphasis of the prophet's message as social justice preaching seems to flow from an under-appreciation of the prophet's role as messengers of God's covenant to God's covenant people. The prophets' prophetic preaching took place within a covenantal context. The social justice issues which the prophets confront are violations of Israel's covenant with God delivered through Moses. "Behind all the indictments and judgments of the prophets lay a broken Sinai covenant."[6] Indeed, judgment was often viewed as a means of purification designed to bring about God's ideal for the community. To summarize Lundbom's description: the prophets' message, comprised of both foretelling and forth-telling, is corrective speech, which addresses social injustice because they always confronted Sinai covenant disobedience.[7]

Returning to the example of the "cows of Bashan," Amos is using very vivid and forceful language to press his point to an audience that has stopped listening to their God. A stern correction or sharp rebuke does not necessarily indicate an absence of shepherding care. Similarly, the preaching pastor must at times "reprove with all authority" (Titus 2:15) conduct which is contrary to Christians' new standing in Christ under the New Covenant. Timothy Oden concludes that rather than the two roles being incompatible, "In this way, Christian preaching stands in continuity with the prophetic tradition."[8]

Since the prophets confronted social justice issues as a matter of covenantal obedience, we must be wary of efforts to use the prophets as a basis for socio-political preaching today. Timothy Sensing points out that because "prophecy is directed to a community in covenant relationship" this "militates against any parallel with modern prophetic preaching directed against a present-day secular state."[9] Political preaching is not prophetic

---

5. Ibid., 28.
6. Lundbom, *The Hebrew Prophets*, 33.
7. Ibid., 32–35.
8. Oden, *Pastoral Theology*, 138.
9. Sensing, "A Call to Prophetic Preaching," 153.

preaching unless it is directed against the kings of Israel or perhaps against errant church leaders.

Another contributing issue that leads to misunderstanding the prophet's message is the social critic's emphasis on the present, to the neglect of the future aspect of prophecy. There is a crucial turn toward hope that is always lingering in the prophets. As Lawrence Boadt says, "there always remained a conviction, even when the prophets used the most absolute and damning language condemning Israel, that God would renew or restore because above all God was faithful."[10] Likewise, Victor Furnish warns against the danger of reducing the prophet's ministry to either champions of social justice or mere predictors of hidden future events:

> "Prophetic preaching" is a term which has been misunderstood in two different directions. Either the prophets have been interpreted as predictors of the future in a very narrow sense (the error of fundamentalism), or else they have been described solely in terms of their criticism of the social and religious structures of their own day (the error of liberalism). Actually, the prophetic word embraced past, present, and future.[11]

Walter Brueggemann concurs; he understands the role of the prophet to be both to *criticize* a dominant social consciousness, which has infected the perception of God's people, and to *energize* the community of faith "to live in fervent anticipation of the newness that God has promised and will surely give."[12] He suggests that conservatives who emphasize future-telling, and liberals who focus on present social injustice, will not balance each other, because both miss the essence of prophetic ministry in ancient Israel and today. For Brueggemann, "The task of prophetic ministry is to nurture, nourish, and evoke a consciousness and perception alternative to the consciousness and perception of the dominant culture around us."[13] Elsewhere, he states, "Thus the old stereotype of 'prophetic' as connoting righteous indignation and rage is at best a partial truth and likely a caricature, because the prophetic books finally concern the future," a future that is beyond the perception of the community at present.[14] Indeed, the same Isaiah who promises the barren will bare numerous children (54:1) and who invites

---

10. Boadt, *Reading the Old Testament*, 550.
11. Furnish, "Prophets, Apostles and Preachers," 49.
12. Brueggemann, *The Prophetic Imagination*, 13.
13. Ibid.
14. Brueggemann, *Introduction to the Old Testament*, 298.

"all who are thirsty, come to the waters" (55:1) is the prophet who also compares his obstinate audience to worthless dogs (56:10) and labels them "the offspring of adulteresses and prostitutes" (57:3). The prophets confront and comfort; they both rage and reassure.

Willimon affirms Brueggemann's conclusions and suggests that "our calls for justice are rarely as critical or as 'prophetic' as we claim them to be because our 'justice' is usually based upon a thoroughly conventional understanding of what is possible within the parameters of present arrangements." He concludes, "Ironically, far from being an attack upon the present order, such preaching is a legitimation of it."[15] Instead of pressuring present realities for the reformation of society, prophetic preaching and pastoral preaching ought to turn our world upside down (Acts 17:6), by proclaiming an alternative reality which has been inaugurated in redemption and will be consummated in Christ's return.

Thus there is a growing body of authors who argue that the key dynamic of prophetic preaching is far more than social criticism; it is bringing both past redemption and future hope to bear on present realities and right living. As Timothy Sensing states:

> The homiletical significance for preachers today is the continuity between God's acts in the past and his acts in the future. It is a reductionistic approach to the literature to see OT prophets as moralistic or legalistic heralds who offer only isolated moral maxims. They always addressed contemporary needs with a word that connected them to their covenant roots and their future hope.[16]

We need to understand the prophets in the full scope of their preaching ministry. They reminded a forgetful people of what God had done for them and of the blessing he had promised them if they would be faithful to his covenant with them.

The prophets applied what God had done for his people in redemption and what God would do in his future restoration to the present dilemmas their audience faced. This aspect of prophetic preaching is directly applicable to pastoral preaching in the church today. Preachers today can rightly apply the prophet's corrective message when we rightly understand the foundation of redemption and the anticipated restoration on which their rebuke and call to repentance is based. Without these essential sideboards,

---

15. Willimon, "Would That All the Lord's People Were Prophets," 18.
16. Sensing, "A Call to Prophetic Preaching," 148.

social justice preaching will not be true "prophetic preaching" at all, but merely politically correct moralizing.

If the prophets indeed preached from a foundation of redemption and with a focus on God's promised restoration, then redemption and hope should be evident themes as we listen in on the prophets' preaching by reading through the prophetic books. The following survey will provide enough of an overview to demonstrate that redemption and hope are prominent in the prophet's preaching. As we listen to the prophets preach repentance and correction based upon redemption and hope, it can help us to make redemption and hope more prominent in our own preaching.

REMEMBERING REDEMPTION

As previously discussed, the preaching of the prophets was rooted in the Torah. Perhaps one of the clearest statements of this is found in Jeremiah 11:1–8:

> The word that came to Jeremiah from the Lord: "Hear the words of this covenant, and speak to the men of Judah and the inhabitants of Jerusalem. You shall say to them, Thus says the Lord, the God of Israel: Cursed be the man who does not hear the words of this covenant that I commanded your fathers when I brought them out of the land of Egypt, from the iron furnace, saying, Listen to my voice, and do all that I command you. So shall you be my people, and I will be your God, that I may confirm the oath that I swore to your fathers, to give them a land flowing with milk and honey, as at this day." Then I answered, "So be it, Lord."
>
> And the Lord said to me, "Proclaim all these words in the cities of Judah and in the streets of Jerusalem: Hear the words of this covenant and do them. For I solemnly warned your fathers when I brought them up out of the land of Egypt, warning them persistently, even to this day, saying, Obey my voice. Yet they did not obey or incline their ear, but everyone walked in the stubbornness of his evil heart. Therefore I brought upon them all the words of this covenant, which I commanded them to do, but they did not."

The prophets spoke to social issues because Israel was under obligation, by covenant with God, to live as his unique people and show his glory among the nations. They were to trust in God, rather than their own armies, or others. They were to live out his divine attributes of righteousness, mercy and humility (Mic 6:8). Even Daniel (although a non-preaching prophet) and his three friends demonstrated a determination to live according to God's covenant (Dan 1:8; 3:18–19). And, as Jeremiah indicates, Israel's unique identity and worship which is prescribed in the covenant consecrated at Sinai, was based upon a singular event: the Exodus, "When I brought them out from the land of Egypt" (Jer 11:4, 7).

This foundational redemptive act is often on the prophet's mind as the basis for his exhortations. The redemption of Israel and the Exodus from Egypt establishes Israel as a unique people of God, in covenant with him as his people, chosen out of all the peoples of the earth (Deut 7:6–8). Their redemption is the basis for their new life and lifestyle as God's people, living in the new life he has given them. When the prophets hold Israel accountable to their covenant with God consecrated at Sinai, that covenant is rooted in their redemption from death and bondage in Egypt through the Passover and the Exodus.

The prophets' foundation of redemption is easily seen in the book of Jeremiah. Immediately following his prophetic call in the first chapter, Jeremiah remembers Israel's redemption from Egypt and God's faithfulness to them through the wilderness in Jeremiah 2:1–9:

> The word of the LORD came to me, saying, "Go and proclaim in the hearing of Jerusalem, Thus says the LORD, "I remember the devotion of your youth, your love as a bride, how you followed me in the wilderness, in a land not sown. Israel was holy to the LORD, the first fruits of his harvest. All who ate of it incurred guilt; disaster came upon them, declares the LORD." Hear the word of the LORD, O house of Jacob, and all the clans of the house of Israel. Thus says the LORD: "What wrong did your fathers find in me that they went far from me, and went after worthlessness, and became worthless? They did not say, 'Where is the LORD who brought us up from the land of Egypt, who led us in the wilderness, in a land of deserts and pits, in a land of drought and deep darkness, in a land that none passes through, where no man dwells?' And I brought you into a plentiful land to enjoy its fruits and its good things. But when you came in, you defiled my land and made my heritage an abomination. The priests did not say, 'Where is the LORD?' Those who handle the law did not know me; the shepherds transgressed against me; the prophets prophesied by Baal and went after things that do not profit. "Therefore I still contend with you, declares the LORD, and with your children's children I will contend.

For Jeremiah, the redemption of Israel from Egypt and God's provision for them through the wilderness are the foundation of their relationship with the Lord (Jer 2:6–9). Israel's failure to live out their covenant relationship with God in light of that redemption is the basis for the Lord's contention with his people through his preaching (Jer 7:21–26; 11:1–5; 32:17–23; 34:13–16).

The foundation of redemption is not as explicit in all the prophets as it is in Jeremiah. Lundbom explains that often the prophets assume the obvious premise, that Israel has forsaken their redeemer and his covenant.[17] The prophets focus on diagnosing the present dilemma in deuteronomic terms, and on the effects this has now brought. Thus, Isaiah's redemptive foundation is more implied than explicit, but is still evident. In his opening chapter Isaiah is clearly confronting God's people in relation to "Israel's covenantal agreement with the Lord,"[18] and that covenant at Sinai is based upon their redemption from Egypt. The high point of Isaiah's covenantal confrontation in chapter one is a redemptive plea for their "sins which are as scarlet" to be made "white as snow" (Isa 1:18). In Isaiah 51:9–11 it is the Lord's redemption of Israel from Egypt that undergirds the hope that he will also redeem them from Babylon. Looking back to Isaiah from our perspective, we can see even more clearly the redemptive foundation to his prophecies: the child Immanuel (Isa 7:14) and the son which will be given (Isa 9:6) are ultimately fulfilled in the incarnation of our Redeemer, Jesus (Mat. 1:23; Luke 2:11). Isaiah's future hope is based upon the redemption of the suffering servant (Isa 53), which has clearly been fulfilled in Jesus (John 12:38; 1 Pet 1:24–25).

During the Babylonian captivity, redemption from Egypt remains a foundational theme for the prophets. In his closing chapters Isaiah gives voice to Israel's prayer for deliverance (Isa 63–65), which repeatedly looks back to the redemption in the Exodus as the basis for their hope that God will again rescue them. When the elders of Israel in Babylon come to Ezekiel for counsel, he rehearses to them Israel's story, which begins with God's making himself known to Israel in Egypt and bringing them out (Ezek 20:5–7). When Daniel perceives that the 70 years prophesied by Jeremiah have nearly passed, his prayer of confession and plea for restoration also remembers God's redemption of Israel (Dan 9:15).

---

17. Lundbom, *The Hebrew Prophets*, 34.
18. Chisholm, *Handbook on the Prophets*, 15.

Part One

Among the Minor Prophets a foundation of redemption and a reference to the covenant based on Israel's redemption from Egypt is also evident. After an attention-grabbing and emotionally impactful introduction (more on that later), Hosea bases his complaint against Israel on their forgetting the Mosaic Covenant (Hos 4:6) and remembers that out of Egypt God called his son Israel (Hos 11:1). Amos confronts Israel for oppressing the poor after God had redeemed them from slavery in Egypt (Amos 2:7–10). The foundation of Amos's complaint against Israel is that they have sinned against the Lord who brought them up out of Egypt and who chose them out of all the people of the earth to be his unique covenant people (Amos 3:1–2). Similarly, Micah's indictment against Israel is based on how the Lord "brought you up from the land of Egypt and redeemed you from the house of slavery . . . that you may know the saving acts of the Lord" (Mic 6:1–5). Habakkuk prays that God will "in wrath remember mercy" (Hab 3:2), and then he poetically rehearses God's great redemptive acts in the Exodus, which give him hope for future redemption (Hab 3:3–19).

Habakkuk is not the only prophet for whom the foundation of redemption is the reference point for their hope of future redemption. Micah remembers God's previous forgiveness (Exod 34:7) as the basis of his hope that "He will again have compassion on us" (Mic 7:18–19). Haggai declares that "the covenant that I made with you when you came out of Egypt" is the foundation for the promise that "Yet once more, in a little while, I will shake the heavens and the earth, the sea and the dry land" (Hag 2:5–6). Thus, the first grand theme of the prophets: *remembering redemption*, leads into their similarly glorious theme: *anticipating hope*.

ANTICIPATING HOPE

The theme of anticipated hope or promised restoration is easily found throughout the prophets. If the prophets were messengers of the covenant who were true to Torah even as they proclaimed further revelation from the Lord, we would expect them to have a message of hope. Moses had spoken both of the disobedience which Israel would fall into as well as the restoration God would bring:

> And when all these things come upon you, the blessing and the curse, which I have set before you, and you call them to mind

among all the nations where the Lord your God has driven you, and return to the Lord your God, you and your children, and obey his voice in all that I command you today, with all your heart and with all your soul, then the Lord your God will restore your fortunes and have compassion on you, and he will gather you again from all the peoples where the Lord your God has scattered you. If your outcasts are in the uttermost parts of heaven, from there the Lord your God will gather you, and from there he will take you. And the Lord your God will bring you into the land that your fathers possessed, that you may possess it. And he will make you more prosperous and numerous than your fathers. And the Lord your God will circumcise your heart and the heart of your offspring, so that you will love the Lord your God with all your heart and with all your soul, that you may live (Deut 30:1–6).

Therefore, it is no surprise that Isaiah speaks of this hope of restoration, in the midst of his opening confrontation, declaring that "it shall come to pass in the latter days that the mountain of the house of the Lord shall be established" and that many peoples will come to it (Isa 2:1–3). In the midst of Ahaz's stubborn refusal to trust the Lord, a promised sign ultimately anticipates Messiah's birth (Isa 7:14). Immediately following the gloomy conclusion to Isaiah 8, he declares that "There will be no more gloom for her who was in anguish," because "the people who walked in darkness have seen a great light . . . for unto us a child is born, to us a son is given and the government shall be upon his shoulder" (Isa 9:1–6). Later, in chapters 40–66, Isaiah assumes the perspective of those already in exile,[19] and so his emphasis moves from an urgent call to repentance to an impassioned plea for the downtrodden people to look to God's promised restoration.

Even Jeremiah, the weeping prophet, is also a messenger of hope. In the presence of evil kings, he declares the Lord "will raise up for David a righteous branch" who will "execute righteousness and justice in the land" and in whose days "Judah will be saved and Israel will dwell securely" (Jer 23:5–6). In the midst of the Babylonian siege of Jerusalem, Jeremiah buys a field and puts the deed in safe keeping for the future, because God will restore his people (Jer 32:1–44). Indeed, it is the weeping prophet who gives the first clear statement of the New Covenant (Jer 31:31–37) which will be inaugurated by Jesus. This New Covenant is the basis for our hope of real and enduring restoration of Israel (and humanity) back to God.

---

19. Chisholm, *Handbook on the Prophets*, 92.

Part One

Similarly Ezekiel, who is known for his graphic portrayals of coming judgment, also gives us one of the most memorable depictions of future resurrection in his vision of the valley of dry bones (Ezek 37:1–28). The same Ezekiel who provided a shocking look at the defilement of the Jerusalem temple as the grounds for God's judgment (Ezek 8:1–18), later gives a detailed description of a future restored temple (Ezek 40–47) which a downtrodden and exiled people look toward in hope.

A quick survey of the Minor Prophets shows this same focus on hope in God's promised restoration. Hosea takes again his wife, ruined, yet restored (Hos 3:1), because those who "are not my people" shall be called "children of the living God" (Hos 1:10–11). Joel anticipates a day when the Lord will pour out his spirit on all flesh (Joel 2:28), and when the Lord will roar from Zion to rescue his people and "Jerusalem will be holy, and strangers shall never again pass through it" (Joel 3:16–17). Amos closes his book anticipating the day when the Lord will "raise up the booth of David that is fallen" and "restore the fortunes of my people Israel" (Amos 9:11, 14). Obadiah concludes his oracle against Edom with a declaration that the exiles of Israel shall possess the land of the Canaanites and the cities of the Negev and "the kingdom shall be the Lord's" (Obad 20–21).

Similarly, Micah declares that Jerusalem will be restored forever (Mic 4:1–7) and that the deliverer will come from little Bethlehem Ephrathah (5:2–4). Because of this, Micah's message of hope is his personal hope: "I will look to the Lord; I will wait for the God of my salvation; my God will hear me" (Mic 7:7). Habakkuk's hope is in the Lord who is in his holy temple (Hab 2:20) and Haggai assures the people that the seemingly little temple they build will one day be filled with a greater glory (Hag 2:7). Zephaniah foresees the day when "the King of Israel, the Lord, is in your midst; you shall never again fear evil" (Zeph 3:15). Zechariah gives a compelling vision of a future pouring out of God's spirit, the cleansing of his people from their sin and the Lord as a warrior king fighting to deliver them and then reigning in their midst (Zech 12–14). Finally, Malachi anticipates the day when the Lord takes up his people as his treasured possession (Mal 3:17), and he declares that as surely the Lord's judgment is coming, so also will he "send you Elijah" to turn their hearts back to him (Mal 4:4–6).

The prophets' anticipation of hope and their proclamation of God's promised restoration is so prominent that the brief survey above will likely remind you of many other examples which I have not included. It is clear that the prophets' preaching remembered redemption and anticipated hope. It should also be noted that the prophets' foundation in redemption and their anticipation of restoration are inseparably tied together. Their future hope is rooted in a greater future redemption they anticipate, which the redemption from Egypt merely prefigures. Jeremiah anticipates a day when the redemption of the Exodus will be overshadowed by a greater salvation of God's people based on the New Covenant (Jer 16:14–15; 23:7–8; 31:31–33).

Yes the prophets preached against rampant social injustice. They boldly confronted contemporary issues their audience faced. They rebuked, corrected and exhorted. But, this was not mere moralistic sermonizing or social critique. The prophets addressed these contemporary issues of righteousness and justice in a covenantal context, urging God's covenant people to live according to the covenant made at Sinai. Furthermore, they did not merely confront moral issues on a moral basis. They addressed Israel and Judah as a redeemed people who were to live in light of the Lord's past redemption and in anticipation of his future restoration. The preaching of the prophets in their present day was solidly anchored between two redemptive realities, one past and one future. In fact, it was these two realities, past and future, redemption and hope, which were the basis for why these people who are God's people should live in a new way. They could and should live for God because he had redeemed them, and they were to live their present lives in light of God's promised future.

PREACHING THE PROPHETS' MESSAGE

There is continuity between the message of preaching prophets and the message of preaching pastors. In churches, Sunday by Sunday, we also preach to an audience largely comprised of God's people, redeemed under the New Covenant. Like the prophets, pastors also preach prophetically when we call the Lord's people to live today in light of their past redemption in Christ and in anticipation of the hope of his coming. We do not urge people to do good for goodness' sake. The Christian life is lived out of God's powerful redemptive working in us. This is the essence of the Apostle Paul's plea in Romans 12:1, "I appeal to you therefore, brothers, by the mercies of God, to present your bodies as a living sacrifice, holy and acceptable to God, which is your spiritual worship." The mercies of God which the Apostle refers to include our justification in Christ's death and resurrection (Rom 3–5), the sanctifying presence and power of the Holy Spirit (Rom

PART ONE

6–8), the certain hope of our glorification (Rom 8:29–39), and the restoration of all things (Rom 9–11).

The prophets urged God's people to live their present, in light of the past and the future. Similarly Paul urges the church to "walk in a manner worthy of the calling to which you have been called" (Eph 4:1). This calling includes both our redemption (Eph 1:7) and a promised inheritance to be fully realized in the future (Eph 1:11–14). Often our redemption is put in language reminiscent of Israel's redemption from Egypt: out of bondage and death into a new life (Eph 2:1–10). At times the comparison is explicit, such as when Paul confronts the immorality in the Corinthian church with a comparison to Passover: "Cleanse out the old that you may be a new lump, as you really are unleavened. For Christ, our Passover lamb, has been sacrificed. Let us therefore celebrate the festival, not with the old leaven, the leaven of malice and evil, but with the unleavened bread of sincerity and truth." (1 Cor 5:7–8). In every one of his epistles, Paul first rehearses and reminds the church of the redemptive truths of "Jesus Christ and him crucified" (1 Cor 2:2), then he unfolds the ethical implications for those who believe the gospel.[20]

This is the pattern given to us in Paul's pastoral instruction to Titus to "teach what accords with sound doctrine" (Tit. 2:1). A lengthy list of moral imperatives follows (2:2–10), which are then grounded in gospel indicatives of redemption and hope:

> For the grace of God has appeared, bringing salvation for all people, training us to renounce ungodliness and worldly passions, and to live self-controlled, upright, and godly lives in the present age, waiting for our blessed hope, the appearing of the glory of our great God and Savior Jesus Christ, who gave himself for

---

20. The same pattern of admonition grounded in accomplished redemption and anticipated hope can also be seen in the evangelistic preaching of the apostles recorded in the book of Acts. Peter borrows from the prophet Joel (Acts 2:17–21), to proclaim forgiveness and the promised restoration (2:38–40). In his second sermon Peter again urges Israel to believe in the forgiveness and hope that is in Jesus (3:13–21) and declares that this is what all the prophets had preached (3:22–26). Paul's sermon at Antioch begins with the Exodus redemption (13:17) and concludes declaring that the blessings of the enduring kingship promised to David are to be fulfilled in Jesus (13:34). These sermons in Acts are evangelistic rather than pastoral exhortation, but the same pattern is also evident when Paul exhorts the elders from Ephesus to continue to "care for the church of God" after his departure (Acts 20:28). Paul's pattern of testifying to "the grace of God" and "proclaiming the kingdom of God" (20:34–35) is the pattern of redemption and hope which he leaves for his successors.

us to redeem us from all lawlessness and to purify for himself a people for his own possession who are zealous for good works (Tit. 2:11–14).

This admonition to renounce worldly passions and to live self-controlled upright and godly lives is secured in the foundation of the salvation bringing gospel and focused toward the glorious appearing of Christ at his return. Paul closes the chapter telling Titus (and other preachers) to "declare these things" (2:15) which includes the imperatives of conduct and also the indicatives of redemption and hope which fuel them.

The apostle models this method in one of his earliest letters. In 1 Thessalonians Paul relates their present labor of love serving the living and true God, to their earlier redemption by faith when they turned to God from idols and their steadfast hope which waits for Jesus's return from heaven (1:3, 9–10). In the following chapters, each admonition is concluded with an expression of prophetic hope in the Lord's return (2:19; 3:13; 4:16–18; 5:23).

Arturo Azurdia provides a good example of Christian pastoral preaching rooted in redemption, rather than mere moralism:

> A preacher, for example, may proclaim to an irresponsible husband, 'You should love your wife in a selfless manner.' At this point, however, he has yet to say anything distinctly Christian. Just as easily could this message have come from John Bradshaw, Harold Kushner, or Louis Farakan. Christian preaching, on the other hand, grounds the ethical imperatives in redemptive indicatives. 'You have a command, dear brother. You must love your wife selflessly. To be sure, this is an awesome task. But consider the following: the source of this command is the Lord Jesus Christ, the model of this command is observed in His own great sacrifice, the strength for this command lies in His purchase of the Holy Spirit, and finally, if disregarded, the encouragement to resume this command is found in the forgiveness He offers because of His work of redemption.[21]

Azurdia's point that moral imperatives grow out of redemptive indicatives is echoed by Bryan Chapell:

> We do what God requires (the imperatives) because we are his people (the indicative relationship his grace alone establishes). We do not become his people by obeying his imperatives. We see ourselves as beloved, beautiful, and precious to him through faith

---

21. Azurdia, *Spirit Empowered Preaching*, 74.

in his redeeming love for us. Thus, preaching that assures God's people that their relationship with him is secure by virtue of God's provision nourishes the faith that becomes the motivation and enablement of true holiness. God's people serve God out of love for him and with confidence of his provision. If preaching purposefully or unintentionally implies that a relationship with God rests on works, then it reverses the biblical order of grace and works, thereby undermining the faith foundations that provide the power of obedience.[22]

Chapell suggests that when Paul grounds his preaching in the cross of Christ, this is a synecdoche "representing the entire matrix of God's redemptive work, past present and future, including the resurrection, advocacy, and reign his victory through the cross provides."[23] Just as the prophets' moral imperatives were bounded by a foundation of redemption and their anticipation of hope, so also our preaching must be bounded by the blessed assurance of redemption in Christ and the blessed hope of Christ's appearing.

Similarly, Graeme Goldsworthy urges preachers to never forget that "in both Testaments, what the people of God are called upon to do is always based upon what has already been done."[24] Gordon Fee has declared that one of the greatest priorities of pastoral ministry is "to help a local body of believers to recapture that New Testament church's understanding of itself as an eschatological community," based on a realization that we live in the end times Christ has already inaugurated, although it is not yet fully realized.[25] Eswine gleans several parallels from the prophets' preaching to ours, including that they "cast a vision for present redemption and future hope."[26]

It is not surprising that something which homileticians consider to be an essential of effective and biblical preaching—an emphasis on redemption and hope—is found in the practice of the prophets. The prophets were effective and biblical preachers. If we desire our preaching to be more "prophetic," the answer is not found merely in focusing more on social justice and other ethical themes we might find the prophets confronted or for which our own culture clamors. Prophetic preaching then and now speaks

22. Chapell, *Christ-Centered Preaching*, 326.
23. Ibid., 278.
24. Goldsworthy, *Preaching the Whole Bible As Christian Scripture*, 6.
25. Fee, *Paul, the Spirit, and the People of God*, 49, quoted in Gordon, "The New Testament in the New Millennium," 56.
26. Eswine, *Preaching to a Post-Everything World*, 122.

the word of God to a contemporary audience, in light of their covenant relationship with God, which is based upon the redemption God has provided and anticipates his promised future.

However, this model does introduce its own tensions. What should be the balance between past redemption and future hope? What should be the balance between the indicatives of redemption and hope and the imperatives of "reproof, correction and for instruction in righteousness" (2 Tim 3:16)? We cannot know this simply from studying the prophets' examples, because their example will vary greatly from prophet to prophet (and audience to audience). This variation among the prophets is divinely directed by the Lord for whom the prophet is merely the messenger. Perhaps an appropriate illustration is to consider the themes of redemption, hope and covenant living as the primary colors of the prophets' palette. The prophets don't merely paint by the numbers. They received divine direction to rightly mix the palette into just the needed shade or hue and to rightly guide the colors to the right place on the canvas, for the Lord's redeemed people are his masterpiece. Preaching pastors also need divine direction in applying redemption and hope to the present challenges faced by the church. The next chapter will show that God has given his Holy Spirit both to the prophets and to preachers to divinely guide them as they proclaim God's truth to God's people.

4

The Spirit of the Lord is Upon Me . . .

But as for me, I am filled with power, with the Spirit of the Lord, and with justice and might, to declare to Jacob his transgression and to Israel his sin.
MICAH 3:8

The Spirit who spoke through the prophets is still speaking today through preaching which passes on the message of God's prophets and apostles.
SIDNEY GREIDANUS[1]

Unless we have the spirit of the prophets resting upon us, the mantle which we wear is nothing but a rough garment to deceive . . . If we have not the Spirit which Jesus promised, we cannot perform the commission which Jesus gave us.
CHARLES HADDON SPURGEON[2]

Often, when men are called to speak God's word as his messenger, they respond with trepidation. This is a calling for which we know that we are not worthy, this is a task for which none of us are adequate. Paul's question echoes in our own hearts, "Who is sufficient for these things?" (2 Cor 2:16). When the Lord called Jeremiah to be his prophet, the young priest protested that he did not "know how to speak, for I am only a youth" (Jer 2:6), but the Lord assured him that he would put his words in the reluctant

---

1. Greidanus, *The Modern Preacher and the Ancient Text*, 8.
2. Spurgeon, *Lectures to My Students*, 187.

prophet's mouth. The divine help God promised to the young prophet, Jeremiah, is the same kind of divine enablement which God gives to his messengers today. This chapter will demonstrate that there is an essential continuity between the Hebrew prophets and Christian pastors: both proclaim the word of God by the Spirit of God. If this is true, then pastors can be encouraged and emboldened in their own preaching by the example of the Spirit-empowered preaching of the prophets.

THE POWER OF THE PROPHETS

The prophet Haggai provides a succinct description of God's messenger faithfully fulfilling his ministry: "Then Haggai, the messenger of the Lord, spoke to the people with the Lord's message, 'I am with you, declares the Lord'" (Hag 1:13). The Lord's messenger gives the Lord's message, and in this case, the message is also true for the prophet. It describes how it is that he can be the Lord's messenger: "I am with you." God promises his enabling presence to the preacher who serves as his messenger. But how does this occur? How is it that the Lord puts his words in the prophet's mouth? How will the Lord be with his messenger? Just as Haggai 1:13 offers a compact definition of the ministry of the prophet, Micah provides a concise statement of the means of the prophet: "But as for me, I am filled with power, with the Spirit of the Lord, and with justice and might, to declare to Jacob" (Micah 3:8). Micah says very explicitly what is implied throughout the prophets, even if it is not very often stated: the prophets speak God's word by God's Spirit. As Lundbom puts it, "To be a prophet is also to be someone filled with the divine Spirit."[3]

Perhaps the prophets do not often state that they spoke the word of the Lord by the Spirit of the Lord because that dynamic was already well established in Israel. For example, even Pharaoh recognized that Joseph spoke God's revelation by God's Spirit (Gen 41:28, 38). The seventy elders of Israel prophesied when the Spirit came upon them (Num 11:25–29). Balaam heard the word of God and prophesied when the Spirit of God came upon him (Num 24:2–4). When the Spirit of God came upon Saul and then on David, they both prophesied to the Israelites (1 Sam 10:10; 19:23; 2 Sam 23:2). Other lesser known prophets such as Azariah, Micaiah, and Jahazial are also described as prophesying when the Spirit of the Lord came upon them (2 Chr 15:1; 18:23; 20:14).

3. Lundbom, *The Hebrew Prophets*, 25.

It may also be that the Hebrew prophets did not make overt claims to their empowerment by the Spirit, in part because of the spiritual ecstasy claimed by false prophets of the region:

> This mark of prophetism is actually played down in the Old Testament. One reason must be the widespread phenomenon of ecstatic prophecy in neighboring cultures. Prophets who showed a tendency to hyper-spirituality often ended up being discredited. This was certainly true in the case of the spirit-filled prophets of Baal, who slashed themselves and performed their rain dance on Mount Carmel (1 Kgs 18:27–29), eliciting nothing but wrath and mockery from Elijah.
>
> There were Hebrew prophets, too, who were judged to possess more "wind" than "spirit." Hosea remarked that "the man of the spirit is mad" (Hos 9:7). Micah claimed that insensitive people in his audience would rather sit and listen to "windy" preachers, who push "liquid spirits" on people, than to his cry against social injustice (Mic 2:11). Jeremiah played on the double meaning of "spirit," saying that some prophets he knows will become what they already are: "bags of wind." The word of Yahweh is not in them (Jer 5:13).[4]

If this is correct, those who speak for God should perhaps be somewhat reluctant to boldly announce their empowerment from on high, lest others think us more "wind bag" than Spirit-filled. James Forbes concurs that many preachers among us shy away from talking about the Spirit's empowerment in preaching because of other's excesses and exaggerated claims in the name of the Spirit.[5] Even Paul demonstrated caution in speaking too strongly about himself and his ministry, "so that no one may think more of me than he sees in me or hears from me" (2 Cor 12:6). We should not need to advertise the Spirit's presence in our preaching; the Lord's presence should be evident in our own lives and in the power of God's word proclaimed by us. At the same time, we should not be "Spirit-shy." We should expect and earnestly seek the Spirit's divine enabling and empowering as those sent by the Lord as his messengers.

---

4. Ibid., 26

5. Forbes, *The Holy Spirit & Preaching*, 22–23.

THE SPIRIT-DEPENDENCE OF PROPHETS AND APOSTLES

It is clear from New Testament references that Israelites in the first century shared an assumed understanding that the prophets spoke by the Holy Spirit.[6] For example, Stephen parallels his antagonists' current resisting of the Holy Spirit to their predecessors who likewise resisted the Spirit when they persecuted the prophets (Acts 7:51). Similarly, Paul declares that the Holy Spirit spoke through Isaiah (Acts 28:25). The author of the epistle to the Hebrews credits the prophetic words of Psalm 95 and the New Covenant prophecy of Jeremiah as the words of the Holy Spirit (Heb 3:7; 10:15). It should not surprise us that "Thus says the Lord" means essentially the same thing as "the Holy Spirit says" (Heb 3:7), since we understand the triune God to exist as Father, Son and Holy Spirit. Therefore, Peter summarizes that "no prophecy was ever produced by the will of man, but men spoke from God as they were carried along by the Holy Spirit" (2 Pet 1:21). We should understand Peter's statement both positively and negatively. Positively, the prophets spoke the word of God by the Spirit of God. Negatively, the Lord's prophets did not presume to speak for God on their own impulse, but only by the Spirit of God.[7]

Just as the New Testament affirms that the Old Testament prophets preached by the Holy Spirit, it also shows that the New Testament apostles and those who followed them in ministry also preached by the divine empowerment of the Holy Spirit. In fact, the Lord's commission to the apostles to preach the gospel was dependent on the promised Spirit to enable them. The moment is recorded in Luke 24:46–49:

> And [Jesus] said to them "Thus it is written, that the Christ should suffer and on the third day rise from the dead, and that repentance and forgiveness of sins should be proclaimed in his name to all nations, beginning from Jerusalem. You are witnesses of these things. And behold, I am sending the promise of my Father upon you. But stay in the city until you are clothed with power from on high."

---

6. Unfortunately, this was not as clear to many rationalist-influenced theologians of the early twentieth century. Spinoza, Schleiermacher, Blake and others reimagined prophetic revelation to be merely human deduction derived from general principles and the prophets' claims of inspiration to be a deceptive rhetorical device. See Heschel, *The Prophets*, 190–205.

7. According to Deuteronomy 18:20–22 the opposite of a true prophet was "the prophet who presumes to speak a word in my name that I have not commanded him to speak."

Jesus declares to them that the gospel of his death and resurrection for forgiveness of sins must be preached, that they are the ones to do it, and he is sending the promised Spirit so that they will have divine power to carry out the mission. Similarly, Acts 1:8 confirms that it is only when they "receive power when the Holy Spirit has come upon you," that they will be his witnesses, effectually proclaiming the gospel. The impact of the Spirit's power is immediately evident when the disciples are filled with the Spirit and begin to speak (Acts 2:4).

SPIRIT-FILLED PREACHERS

The phrase "filled with the Holy Spirit" occurs nine times in Luke and Acts. In each of these instances, the filling of the Spirit is God's provision for effectively carrying out the commission to proclaim the gospel. These instances show that the Spirit's filling forms a bridge of continuity between the last of the Old Testament prophets, John the Baptist, and the earliest preachers in the church era, Peter and Paul. As the baton was passed from Old Testament prophet to New Covenant preacher, the testimony of Jesus by the power of the Spirit was their common link. "The Holy Spirit's empowerment (anointing) serves as the common denominator of proclamation in both Testaments, solidly grounding Spirit-led preaching in the biblical witness."[8]

The first occurrence of the phrase *filled with the Holy Spirit* refers to John the Baptist who will be filled with the Spirit in order that he may, as the forerunner of Jesus, "make ready for the Lord a people prepared" (Luke 1:15–17). Elizabeth, John's mother, is *filled with the Spirit* when Mary comes to visit her, and she immediately speaks prophetically to Mary concerning the unborn Christ (Luke 1:41–43). John's father, Zechariah, is *filled with the Spirit* and immediately speaks prophetically of the Lord's salvation and redemption in the Son of David, even before speaking of the ministry of his own son John (Luke 1:67). Moving on to the book of Acts, immediately after all the disciples are *filled with the Spirit* and speak of God's mighty works (Acts 2:4, 11), Peter exposits the Old Testament scriptures to clearly and boldly proclaim Jesus as the Christ, crucified and risen for the forgiveness of sins (Acts 2:14–40). Next, Peter and John, *filled with the Spirit*, boldly declare Jesus to the council of Jewish rulers, priests and elders (Acts 4:8–12).

8. Heisler, *Spirit-Led Preaching*, 26.

The next occurrence of Spirit-filling became especially personal to me one evening during my years of missionary service when I was meeting with a church mission team. After concluding the various business and reports, the team members prayed for the witness and ministry of each of the church's missionaries. Just after our prayers were concluded and we rose to our feet, the house began to shake from a moderately strong earthquake. Waiting within the shelter of a doorway for the tremor to subside, I was reminded of Peter and John's return to the other disciples following their interrogation by the council. They prayed for the Lord to help them "continue to speak the word with boldness" (Acts 4:29). "And when they had prayed, the place in which they were gathered together was shaken, and they were all *filled with the Holy Spirit* and continued to speak the word of God with boldness" (Acts 4:31).

Next, Saul (Paul) is told that he will be *filled with the Spirit* to "carry my name before the Gentiles and kings and the children of Israel" (Acts 9:10–17). Paul is later specifically said to be *filled with the Spirit* when he spoke to the magician on Cyprus (Acts 13:9). Finally, at Antioch in Pisidia, Paul proclaims that God has made Jesus "a light for the Gentiles that you may bring salvation to the ends of the earth." The Gentiles receive this word gladly and after this episode of Paul's preaching the epilogue is written, "The disciples were filled with joy and *with the Holy Spirit*" (Acts 13:47–52). Consistently in Luke and Acts, the filling of the Spirit is directly related to proclaiming the gospel of Jesus Christ. What was essential for the prophets is also foundational for the early church: it is by the filling of the Spirit that Jesus is effectively proclaimed.

Arturo Azurdia provides a similar survey of these incidents of Spirit-filling in Luke and Acts and concludes that the filling of the Spirit is distinct from the Spirit's continual indwelling of each and every believer.[9] In each of these instances "the filling of the Spirit is presented as an *event*, a sovereign and spontaneous act of God related to the proclamation of truth."[10] While it is true that every born-again believer is indwelt by the Holy Spirit, the filling of the Spirit should not be taken for granted. It is evident that we should not assume that all Christians are filled with the Spirit by the fact that we are commanded to "be filled with the Spirit" (Eph 5:18). The imperative mood and passive voice of the verb "be filled" show that "it is

---

9. Azurdia, *Spirit Empowered Preaching*, 102–7. I am especially indebted to Dr. Azurdia in this chapter.

10. Ibid., 103.

Part One

'by the Spirit' that God's people are filled. At the same time believers, both individually and corporately, are to be wholly and utterly involved in this process of infilling."[11] The present tense of the verb suggests that "believers' experience of the Spirit's fullness is to be a continuing one."[12]

But how is the Spirit's filling both a spontaneous event with immediate effect, while also being a continuous experience? Hoehner clarifies that the present tense should be understood to have an iterative force, a repeated action,[13] which is also evident in the apostles' reoccurring Spirit-filling recorded in the book of Acts. So then, we can conclude that those who proclaim the gospel should give continuing attention to being filled by the Spirit.

But, what does it mean to be filled with the Spirit? In Ephesians 5:18 Paul provides a helpful illustration of being filled with the Spirit as being under the fruitful and effectual influence of the Spirit, rather than the degrading influence of wine or other intoxicants. The Spirit's filling is juxtaposed with the debauchery of reduced inhibitions to sin from being "drunk with wine." In contrast, the Sprit's filling is evidenced by worshipful singing, giving thanks, and mutual submission (Eph 5:19–21).[14] Being filled with wine might lead a man to foolishly say something he might not otherwise say. Similarly, being filled with the Spirit might lead a man to wisely say something he would not otherwise say (or say wisely). Imagine the damage that could be done to the church if the preacher was drunk in the pulpit. This image, in contrast, can help us to see the blessing which can come to the church when the preacher is filled by the Spirit when preaching.

Spurgeon considered the Spirit's divine influence and enablement to be essential for preaching: "A preacher ought to know that he really possesses the Spirit of God, and that when he speaks there is an influence upon him that enables him to speak as God would have him, otherwise out of the pulpit he should go directly; he has no right to be there, he has not been called to preach God's truth."[15]

This Spirit-filling includes the divine impartation of ability, intelligence, knowledge and skill needed for the task to which God has called

11. O'Brien, *Ephesians*, 393.

12. Lincoln, *Ephesians*, 344. See also Wallace, *Greek Grammar Beyond the Basics*, 374–75.

13. Hoehner, *Ephesians*, 704.

14. It could be argued that since Ephesians 5:22 is dependent or in "submission" to 5:21, the fruit of the filling of the Spirit is also evident in marriage, family and occupational relationships.

15. Bacon, *Spurgeon*, 82.

The Spirit of the Lord is Upon Me ...

someone (Exod 31:3; 35:31). In the instances described above by Luke in the book of Acts, Spirit-filling appears to include insight into God's word (Acts 2:4–36), as well as insight to spiritually discern the needs of the occasion in which the word of God is proclaimed (Acts 4:8; 13:9). Spirit-filling divinely enables the preacher to know what to say and how to say it. Hoehner summarizes:

> The filling by the Spirit is more than the Spirit's indwelling—it is his activities realized in and through us. Believers are commanded to be filled by the Spirit so that they will understand the will of the Lord and allow God's control of their lives, thus providing enablement to make the most of every opportunity, rather than succumbing to the desires of the flesh.[16]

To understand the meaning and purpose of the filling of the Spirit, the use of πληρόω, *pleroō*, to fill, must be understood in terms of its other occurrences in Ephesians. The church, the body of Christ is the fullness of him [Christ] who *fills* all in all (Eph 1:23), and believers are to be *filled* with all the fullness of God (Eph 3:19). Jesus ascended "that he might *fill* all things" (Eph 4:10) so that ultimately the church may "attain the measure of the stature of the fullness of Christ" (Eph 4:13). This last phrase refers to the church maturing, growing up into, and attaining to the complete realization of all that it already is as the fullness of Christ.[17] To summarize, the church is the fullness of Christ (1:23), so prayer is made for believers to be filled with the fullness of God in their experience (3:19), so that through the ministry of spirit-gifted preachers (4:11), the church would corporately realize her identity as the fullness of Christ (4:13). To this end we are individually commanded to be filled by the Spirit (5:18).

To restate it more plainly, the filling of the Spirit is the empowering presence of God within the believer to bring to fulfillment the maturity of Christ-likeness in believers individually and the church corporately. Ephesians 4:10–16 makes clear that this maturing and Spirit filling of believers in the body of Christ is accomplished through the means of the Spirit-filled preaching of the word of God through those gifted and given to the church by the Lord through the Spirit. The church as a whole is blessed and benefited by preachers of the word who have been given a specific gifting by the Holy Spirit to preach under the influence of, and in the power of, the Holy Spirit.

16. Hoehner, *Ephesians*, 705.
17. Lincoln, *Ephesians*, 257. See also Hoehner, *Ephesians*, 703–5.

Part One

PREACHING WITH POWER

This dependence on the Spirit for the fruitfulness in his preaching is clearly evident in Paul's ministry, but perhaps nowhere more so than in his correspondence with the church in Corinth, where they were so fond of eloquent orators. Referring to the preaching of himself and others, Paul summarized where the power for fruitful results from preaching resides: "I planted, Apollos watered, but God caused it to grow" (1 Cor 3:6). Paul declared that without the insight and illumination given by the Spirit, no one would comprehend the gospel:

> Now we have received not the spirit of the world, but the Spirit who is from God, that we might understand the things freely given us by God. And we impart this in words not taught by human wisdom but taught by the Spirit, interpreting spiritual truths to those who are spiritual. The natural person does not accept the things of the Spirit of God, for they are folly to him, and he is not able to understand them because they are spiritually discerned (1 Cor 2:12, 14).

Paul credits the empowering of the Spirit for his own insight into God's message, for the very words he chooses to proclaim it, and for the effectual power of his preaching in the lives of those who hear. This seems to be what Paul refers to when he declares, "My conversation and my preaching were not with persuasive words of wisdom, but with a demonstration of the Spirit and of power, so that your faith would not be based on human wisdom but on the power of God" (1 Cor 2:4–5, NET).

The phrase "demonstration of the Spirit and of power" is sometimes thought to refer to authenticating miracles which accompanied Paul's preaching and which caused his message to be believed. However, this would be contrary to Jesus's declaration that miracles will not help if God's word is not believed: "If they do not hear Moses and the Prophets, neither will they be convinced if someone should rise from the dead" (Luke 16:31). The Greek word ἀποδείξει, *apodéixei*, translated *demonstration* "is a technical term in rhetoric for 'proof' from a verbal demonstration. But in this case the proof did not come from rhetorical persuasion; it came from God."[18] The two words, "demonstration and power," most likely form a hendiadys and refer to the conviction of the Holy Spirit through Paul's preaching lead-

---

18. Garland, 1 *Corinthians*, 87. See also Kistemaker, *Exposition of the First Epistle to the Corinthians*, 76.

ing to their conversion.[19] Azurdia summarizes the lexical and grammatical evidence and concludes that Paul's preaching "was characterized not by manipulative techniques of communication, but by a supernatural verification that was supplied by the power of the Spirit of God."[20] Paul describes the Spirit's convincing power of his preaching to the Thessalonians in similar terms: " . . . our gospel came to you not only in word, but also in power and in the Holy Spirit and with full conviction" (1 Thess 1:5).

In the New Testament era effective preaching is proclaiming God's word "by the Holy Spirit" (1 Pet 1:12). George Kennedy summarizes the continuity from the prophets to Christian preachers as far as their similar dependence on the Holy Spirit for persuasive effect:

> Some practical recognition is given to natural ability, but the Judeo-Christian orator, at least in theory, has little need of practice or knowledge of an art as required by the orator in the classical tradition. He needs only the inspiration of the Spirit. The role of the speaker in Judeo-Christian rhetoric is generally incidental . . . Persuasion takes place when God is ready.
>
> Similarly in Christian rhetoric God must act, through his grace, to move the hearts of an audience before individuals can receive the Word, and if he does pour out this grace, the truth of the message will be recognized because of its authority, and not through its logical argumentation.[21]

This, then, is the lesson that Christian preachers must learn from the ministry of the prophets. We should be reluctant, even fearful of preaching in our own strength or in the confidence of our own rhetorical eloquence and effectiveness. We, like the prophets, are desperately dependent on the Holy Spirit. Robert Smith points out our need of the Spirit's empowerment with the most compelling example possible:

> If Jesus the Son of God, the infinite One, the sender of the Holy Spirit to the church on the day of Pentecost, declared that the Spirit of the Lord was upon Him to preach, can we preachers, who are frail, weak, and finite vessels, settle for anything less? To see the work of God demonstrated in our preaching necessitates the indwelling power of the Holy Spirit.[22]

---

19. Fee, *God's Empowering Presence*, 92.
20. Azurdia, *Spirit Empowered Preaching*, 100.
21. Kennedy, *Classical Rhetoric*, 122–23.
22. Smith, foreword to Heisler, *Spirit-Led Preaching*, xii.

Smith is alluding to Jesus's appropriation of Isaiah 61:1–2 to himself. In Isaiah 61:1–11 the prophet voices the words of the coming anointed one, whom Jesus identified as himself (Luke 4:18–19). It might seem an overstatement to apply the same anointing language to preachers today, except that Joel prophesied of a day when the Spirit would be poured out on all (Joel 2:28–29).[23] Forbes shows that the apostles used the same anointing language to refer to all Christians:

> In II Corinthians 1:21–22, Paul says, "Now he which establisheth us with you in Christ and hath anointed us is God, who hath also sealed us and given the earnest of the Spirit in our hearts" (KJV). The other specific references occur in I John 2:20, 27. I John 2:20 says, "But you have been anointed by the Holy One, and you all know." Verse 27 repeats the term: "but the anointing which you received from him abides in you, and you have no need that anyone should teach you; as his anointing teaches you about everything, and is true, and is no lie, just as it has taught you, abide in him."[24]

Forbes suggests that the early church did not overtly use the term "anointed" to describe themselves, aware of the kingly connotations it could have to Rome, as well as in deference to the uniqueness of Jesus as the Christ, "The Anointed." He suggests that the terms they did use more commonly, referring to the *filling* and the *power* of the Spirit, had at least a similar connotation among the early church as the anointing of Luke 4:18–19.[25] Greidanus affirms that there is a technical difference but also an essential continuity between the Spirit-inspired messengers of the Old and New Testament writings and the Spirit-illumined messengers of God's word today:

> Some have sought to articulate the difference between the biblical preachers and their contemporary counterparts as follows: "The Old Testament and the New Testament organs of revelation came forward saying: 'Thus Says the Lord.' . . . But the New Testament preacher must say, if he would speak strictly: 'Thus has the Lord written.'" Technically, in terms of the source of revelation, this formulation is correct, but materially, in terms of the reality of God's word, contemporary preachers should also be able to say: 'Thus says the Lord." For the Spirit who spoke through the prophets is

---

23. Forbes, *The Holy Spirit and Preaching*, 29.
24. Ibid., 44.
25. Ibid.

still speaking today through preaching which passes on the message of God's prophets and apostles.[26]

Whatever terms we are comfortable using—filling, power, anointing—we are certainly as dependent upon the empowering of the Holy Spirit for fruitful and effectual ministry as the apostles and prophets who preceded us. We are rightly cautious to claim for ourselves the same kind or category of empowering which Paul could claim as an apostle. However, in these instances (1 Cor 2:4, 1 Thess. 1:5) Paul does not seem to be referring to specific power or signs unique to an apostle as he does elsewhere (2 Cor 12:12). Paul uses these terms to describe his regular public preaching and individual conversations, the same kind of ministry pastors continue today. In fact, Paul seems quite like us when he asks the Ephesian church to pray for all believers and for him, that he would have boldness to proclaim the gospel as he should (Eph 6:18–19). Azurdia links this prayer for boldness to the similar prayer in Acts 4:29–31, and summarizes the filling of the Spirit in this way: "When the Holy Spirit powerfully attends the preaching of the word of God there is an ease of speaking, a holy authority, another-worldly kind of courage that can compel an ordinary man to invade the domain of darkness and demand the deliverance of people enslaved to that realm."[27]

I am one of those whom Azurdia refers to as an ordinary man. In a day when the gospel and its preachers are increasingly marginalized in society, and perhaps at times intimidated by society, I need this boldness beyond myself. We need courage which the Holy Spirit powerfully gives to faithfully proclaim God's word.

NEW COVENANT ILLUMINATION

Perhaps the greatest argument for Christian preachers' dependency on and empowerment by the Holy Spirit is the fact that we are participants in and ministers of the New Covenant. The essence of the New Covenant (Jer 31:31–34) is the promise of the indwelling and empowering Spirit: "I will give you a new heart, and a new spirit I will put within you. And I will remove the heart of stone from your flesh and give you a heart of flesh. And I will put my Spirit within you" (Ezek 36:26–27). Paul spoke of God's transforming work in the lives of those he preached to as God's written

---

26. Greidanus, *The Modern Preacher and the Ancient Text*, 8.
27. Azurdia, *Spirit Empowered Preaching*, 122.

PART ONE

letter of recommendation, "written not with ink but with the Spirit of the living God, not on tablets of stone but on tablets of human hearts" (2 Cor 3:3). Paul credits the Spirit of God as the one who empowers preachers of the gospel: "Not that we are sufficient in ourselves to claim anything as coming from us, but our sufficiency is from God, who has made us competent to be ministers of a new covenant, not of the letter but of the Spirit. For the letter kills, but the Spirit gives life" (2 Cor 3:5–6). Because it is the Spirit who gives life and transforms lives (2 Cor 3:18), Paul's confidence for effectual preaching comes from the Spirit's power and presence in the clear proclamation of God's word, not by any manipulative methods (2 Cor 4:1–2). Because blindness to the gospel is a spiritual problem (2 Cor 4:3–4), God, by his Spirit, must illumine the gospel to their hearts. Preachers are merely weak vessels, for "the surpassing power belongs to God and not to us" (2 Cor 4:6–7). Thus we preach the New Covenant message of forgiveness of sins by the New Covenant means of the indwelling and empowering Holy Spirit.

The need for God's Spirit to illumine the word of God is not only true concerning the audience. The preaching pastor also needs the illumination of God's Spirit:

> These things God has revealed to us through the Spirit. For the Spirit searches everything, even the depths of God. For who knows a person's thoughts except the spirit of that person, which is in him? So also no one comprehends the thoughts of God except the Spirit of God. Now we have received not the spirit of the world, but the Spirit who is from God, that we might understand the things freely given us by God. And we impart this in words not taught by human wisdom but taught by the Spirit, interpreting spiritual truths to those who are spiritual. (1 Cor 2:10–13).

We need the illumination of the Spirit in order to understand the revelation of God which was given by the inspiration of the Spirit. As Heisler says, "Illumination is a continuing work of the Spirit that guides us into all truth (John 16:13). This means that the Spirit's illumination is the guide to his inspiration, and we desperately need his guidance into truth because we are sinful, fallen, and fallible human beings."[28] John MacArthur describes the necessity of the Spirit's illumination for both the preacher and the congregation:

---

28. Heisler, *Spirit-Led Preaching*, 41.

> Powerful preaching occurs only when a Spirit-illumined man of God expounds clearly and compellingly the Spirit-inspired revelation in Scripture to a spirit-illumined congregation ... Illumination is the work of the Holy Spirit that opens one's spiritual eyes to comprehend the meaning of the Word of God. It involves the preacher of Scripture and his audience. God's objective and historically past revelation in Scripture cannot be understood accurately apart from the present, personal and subjective work of the Holy Spirit.[29]

The illumination of the Spirit does not eliminate the need for preachers to study and prepare, diligently digging into the text with the help of dictionaries, lexicons, grammars, and commentaries. MacArthur gives the example of Luke, who "investigated everything carefully from the beginning" (Luke 1:3) before writing his Gospel. He concludes: "If human effort was a component in inspiration, how much more is the need for diligent study in conjunction with illumination."[30] Roy Zuck warns against reliance on the illumination of the Spirit as an excuse for neglecting diligent preparation: "Depending on the Holy Spirit in one's teaching does not mean being unprepared and 'simply letting the Holy Spirit speak through me,' as if preparation competed with spirituality. Just the opposite is true. Unpreparedness is not a sign of being 'more spiritual.'"[31]

Most importantly, preachers are dependent on the illumination of the Spirit in ways similar to the prophets' dependence on the Spirit because both prophets and preachers are more than mere messengers mouthing words. Prophets and preachers speak God's word with God's heart. Heschel puts it very well:

> The prophetic speeches are not factual pronouncements. What we hear is not objective criticism or the cold proclamation of doom. The style of legal, objective utterance is alien to the prophet. He dwells upon God's inner motives, not only upon His historical decisions. He discloses a divine pathos, not just a divine judgment. The pages of the prophetic writings are filled with echoes of divine love and disappointment, mercy and indignation. The God of Israel is never impersonal ...
>
> The prophet is not a mouthpiece, but a person; not an instrument, but a partner, an associate of God ...

---

29. MacArthur, *Preaching*, 78.
30. Ibid., 82.
31. Zuck, "The Role of The Holy Spirit in Christian Teaching," 34.

> . . . the task of the prophet is to convey the word of God. Yet the word is aglow with the pathos. One cannot understand the word without sensing the pathos. And one could not impassion others and remain unstirred. The prophet should not be regarded as an ambassador who must be dispassionate in order to be effective.[32]

Thus Timothy Sensing concludes: "Prophets experienced a fellowship with the feelings of God. They shared a sympathy with the divine pathos. Prophets were in touch with the heart of God; therefore, they expressed God's heart as God's voice. Prophets imparted God's heart together with its content."[33] It is commonly understood that passion is far more effective in preaching than indifference. Still, we dare not use emotion or passion merely as a rhetorical technique. When we communicate God's truth, we must also convey God's passion. This best occurs when the preacher is filled by the Spirit and thus burdened by the Spirit's burden. We cannot get there without the Spirit because only "the Spirit searches everything, even the depths of God . . . so also no one comprehends the thoughts of God except the Spirit of God" (1 Cor 2:10–11). If we cannot understand the truth of God's word without the illumination of the Spirit, we are even more dependent on the Spirit to know and express the heart and pathos of God.

SPIRIT-FILLED PREACHING TODAY

The prophets revealed the person of God through the word of God, by the Spirit or God. Today preachers are called to do the same. As James Forbes has said, a "spirited pastor will not suffice" we need the power of the Spirit.[34] Therefore we exhort ourselves with the same exhortation we proclaim to the church: "Be filled with the Spirit" (Eph 5:18).

To be filled by the Spirit comes from a preacher himself being yielded to the Spirit. Haddon Robinson, in his time-tested definition for expository preaching, includes the application of the word by the Spirit to the preacher: "Expository preaching is the communication of a biblical concept, derived from and transmitted through a historical, grammatical, and literary study of a passage in its context, *which the Holy Spirit first applies to the personality and experience of the preacher*, then through him to his

---

32. Heschel, *The Prophets*, 22–26.
33. Sensing, "A Call to Prophetic Preaching," 144.
34. Forbes, *The Holy Spirit & Preaching*, 25.

hearers" (emphasis mine).[35] Robinson is convinced that "ultimately God is more interested in developing messengers than messages" and that preaching is more about making a preacher than making a sermon. Thus, "true preaching comes when the loving heart and the disciplined mind are laid at the disposal of the Holy Spirit."[36] So as faithful preachers we pray: Lord, I want you to work through me, so I need you to work in me.

For further clarity, there are some biblical corollaries to the positive command for us to be filled by the Spirit: we are to guard against grieving the Spirit (Eph 4:30) and quenching the Spirit (1 Thess. 5:19). The command, "and do not grieve the Holy Spirit of God, by whom you were sealed for the day of redemption" occurs in the midst of a collection of admonitions (Eph 4:25–32), which all seem to delineate what it is to be "renewed in the spirit of your minds and put on the new self, created after the likeness of God in true righteousness and holiness" (Eph 4:24). Grieving the Spirit can be summarized as stubbornly refusing to respond to and live out God's grace in life's choices. Israel "grieved the Lord" when they did not live in his redemption and the new life in the covenant he made with them (Ps 78:40–58; Isa 63:7–10). In the same way we grieve the Lord today when we as preachers do not ourselves live in the implications of the gospel we preach. Robinson is right—the word of God must first be applied to the preacher before it can effectively be applied through him to the congregation.

Zack Eswine warns preachers of several ways in which we can grieve the Spirit and quench his power.[37] He warns us against preaching morality and our own precepts instead of Christ, and of failing to boldly declare what God has said in his word. These will quench the Spirit's power in our preaching. He warns against feebleness or carelessness in our own personal devotional life which will also open the way to increased vulnerability to the devil's temptations. He urges men of God to cultivate spiritual discipline without allowing it to become religious routine. We must "meet personally with God, not just professionally."[38] One of the best ways in which we can serve the Lord in our preaching ministry and be used by him to feed his flock, is to draw near to him in his fellowship and forgiveness in Christ (1 John 1:3–10). Like every person we preach to, we also continue to need to

---

35. Robinson, *Biblical Preaching*, 21.
36. Barclay, *A Spiritual Biography*, 27.
37. Eswine, *Preaching to a Post-everything World*, 253–66.
38. Ibid., 262.

hear God's comfort and his confrontation, and draw nearer to our Lord in the yielded repentance which genuine faith produces.

As I come to the end of this chapter, it's Saturday evening; tomorrow I will be preaching Psalm 2. It's a glorious prophetic text, which exalts Christ and is extremely relevant to the times in which we live. Tomorrow, through the preaching of this word, guests among us could be joined to "those who take refuge in him" (Ps 2:12). Believers could be strengthened and emboldened to "serve the Lord with fear and rejoice with trembling" (Ps 2:11), because they receive a clearer glimpse of "He who sits in the heavens" (Ps 2:4). I believe this is going to be a very good sermon, and yet it may be that none of that happens. I can't make any of it happen, for none of it is ultimately dependent upon how well I preach; all is dependent on the working of the Holy Spirit. It is the Spirit who inspired the text through the prophet, who illumines the pastor in the study, who enlightens the understanding of the congregation, and who powerfully works to open the heart and mind of the unbeliever.

Recently, a woman in our congregation came to me just before the worship service began and wanted me to know that she prays for me every week. She told me that she prays for me in my studying and before I preach, and she prays that the church will hear God's word with understanding and compelling conviction. This woman also prays that people who have not yet come to faith in Christ might hear and believe the gospel through the message today. She told me she is grateful that she perceives an increasing reliance on the Holy Spirit in our church. I am grateful that our church is blessed with this woman of simple faith and persistent prayer. Lord, hear her prayers, and those of countless others like her!

May the prophets, who dared not speak apart from the Spirit of God, encourage us to continue this ministry of proclaiming God's word by the power of God's Spirit. May we be encouraged to faithfully fulfill our ministry, knowing that the confidence of the prophets can also be the confidence of preachers: "the Spirit of the Lord is upon me . . ."

Part Two

5

Opening Words and Opening Ears

It is the same with men as with donkeys, whoever would hold them fast must get a good grip on their ears.

RUSSIAN PROVERB

The assumption that one's listeners automatically share one's own interest in the sermon is a mark of an inexperienced preacher.

BRYAN CHAPELL[1]

In the previous chapters we have considered significant continuities between the Hebrew prophets and Christian preachers. As preachers we do not claim the prophet's mantle, but we can claim significant parallels between our preaching and the preaching of the prophets. Preachers have the same essential ministry as prophets: we speak the word of God to God's people. We also have a similarly framed message: we apply the Lord's previous redemption and promised hope to present life situations. Furthermore, both prophets and preachers carry out their glorious ministry by the same essential means: the Spirit of the Lord is upon us. In light of these significant continuities between the prophets and preachers, we should expect there to be some continuity between how the prophets preached and how we ought to preach. The following chapters will explore some of the preaching methodology or rhetoric of the prophets, as described in recent literature in the field of Old Testament rhetorical analysis. We will compare the rhetoric of

---

1. Chapell, *Christ-Centered Preaching*, 238.

Part Two

the prophets to current preaching theory to see what preachers today might learn from the preaching of the prophets.

LEARNING FROM THE PROPHETS' PREACHING

Further consideration of the rhetoric of the prophets has been called for by students of Old Testament rhetorical criticism, including David Howard who suggests that Old Testament studies would "benefit greatly from self-consciously focusing upon the speeches and other discourse in the Bible with an eye to discerning the means of persuasion practiced, bringing to bear insights from the study of rhetoric which has long been known as 'rhetorical criticism.'"[2] Howard is calling for more than the mere cataloging of rhetorical devices; he is urging a more careful examination of the rhetorical technique applied by the prophets as a means of persuasion.[3] This is important because at "its heart, preaching is about persuasion."[4]

My goal is to show that the prophets can be helpful examples of pastoral preaching of God's word to God's people, in order to encourage preachers to notice from the prophets not only what they say, but how they say it. The prophets themselves appear to have learned from, or were at least aware of, their predecessors: "They were not lone individualists who knew nothing and cared nothing for what others who bore the name 'prophet' had said. Rather, they saw themselves in a line of succession and were aware of the tradition they had received from their predecessors."[5] Therefore, following their example, we should also learn from the prophets as our preaching predecessors.

The prophets are worth learning from because, as Lessing says, "their sermons are unsurpassed in visionary scope, moral insight, and imaginative impact. This is so because, to a great extent, the prophets used rhetorical

---

2. Howard "Rhetorical Criticism in Old Testament Studies," 103.

3. Ibid., 88. For a helpful historical survey of developments in Old Testament rhetorical criticism see Wuellner, "Where is Rhetorical Criticism Taking Us?" 448–63. Wuellner discusses how rhetorical criticism became "rhetoric restrained" by attention focused on literary forms and styles at the expense of consideration given to the persuasive force or effect of the rhetorical style or device employed. For a survey of developments in Old Testament literary criticism, see Muilenburg, "Form Criticism and Beyond," and Cook, "Beyond 'Form Criticism and Beyond.'"

4. Lybrand, *Preaching on your Feet*, 27.

5. Bullock, *An Introduction to the Old Testament Prophetic Books*, 13.

strategies in highly effective ways."[6] Paying attention to the rhetoric of the prophets can help today's preachers become clearer, more memorable, more relevant and more persuasive in their preaching. Lundbom notes that all of the prophets "possessed rhetorical skills that are worthy of our attention," and he suggests that we can learn "a considerable amount by simply reading the biblical text with an eye for the rhetorical nature of its discourse."[7] Lessing suggests that preachers can and should "learn from the prophet's homiletical moves, structures, and strategies."[8] We should take notice of the prophet's rhetorical skills, not so that we might artificially emulate them, but that they might inspire us to be more effective in our own communication of God's word.

A RHETORIC OF ENTRAPMENT

The prophets carefully constructed their speech in order to "prepare the audience to hear the thesis, to refute opposing views, and then to wrap the address up with the main points and application."[9] Often what they had to say was hard to hear, and they needed to prepare the audience to hear it. An excellent example of a captivating introduction which prepares the audience for the main point of the message is found in the first two chapters of the prophet Amos. Amos was bringing a message of judgment to Israel which his audience would not want to hear or accept.[10] Amos, like Nathan coming to David (2 Sam 12:1–12), begins his sermon with an introduction which will open his audience up to his message before they see it coming.

The book of Amos begins with a series of brief oracles against the nations in Amos chapters 1 and 2 which pose a problem for the interpreter. "What was the need to speak of or to nations that could not hear and consequently could not respond to the prophet's warning or word of judgment"?[11] Many commentators seem to give equal weight to Amos's oracles against Syria, Philistia, Tyre, Edom, Ammon, Moab, and Judah as they do to the final oracle against Israel. The oracles against the nations are often taken as introductory to Amos's prophecy against Israel (which concludes chap-

---

6. Lessing, "Preaching like the Prophets," 391.
7. Lundbom, *The Hebrew Prophets*, 168, 165.
8. Lessing, "Orality in the Prophets," 153.
9. Lessing, "Preaching like the Prophets," 400.
10. Smith, *The Prophets As Preachers*, 47.
11. Bullock, *An Introduction to the Old Testament Prophetic Books*, 79.

PART TWO

ter 2 and continues throughout the book), mainly in the sense that they depict the universality and impartiality of God's judgment.[12] Some of these authors do acknowledge some rhetorical aspects of these oracles. For example, Bullock suggests that the "oracles against the nations obviously had a cumulative effect whose sum was the absolutely inescapable judgment of Israel." Stuart refers to the geographical order of the list that seems to intentionally locate Judah, then Israel, in the center.[13] The effect is something like an artillery gunner, tightening his trajectory and slowly but surely zeroing in on his true target. It is apparent that there is some introductory aspect to these oracles, in that they do bring the message forward to its intended focus on Israel. However, more in-depth rhetorical analysis has revealed an even more detailed and specific climactic effect of these introductory oracles: they are intentionally devised to draw Amos's audience toward agreement with his disagreeable message.

The unifying feature of the oracles is the formulaic introduction of each one: "For three sins . . . even for four." However, in each of the first seven oracles, neither three nor four sins are enumerated. Each oracle condemns one or perhaps two offenses and then hurries on without fully developing the three sins or four.[14] Robert Chisholm describes how the incompletion of the "three, even four" formula moves the audience toward the main point, which is God's condemnation of Israel:

> A close reading of the oracles shows that the prophet was hinting at this all along. Each of the oracles begins with the formula "For three sins of [name of city or state], even for four, I will not turn back my wrath." Based on structural parallels with proverbial statements that use the "three, even four" numerical pattern (see Prov 30:15–16, 18–19, 21–23, 29–31), one expects to find a list of four specific sins in each oracle. But this never happens in the first seven oracles. After specifying one or two sins, the prophet breaks

---

12. For instance, see: Feinberg, *The Minor Prophets*, 86–91; Sunukjian, "Amos," 1427–31; Stuart, *Hosea-Jonah*, 308; Brueggemann, *An Introduction to the Old Testament*, 257.

13. Stuart, *Hosea-Jonah*, 310–15.

14. It may appear that multiple sins are enumerated for each, but Chisholm has shown that while in a formal sense, multiple offenses are listed, parallelisms in each oracle are actually describing one conceptual sin (or perhaps two) in each of the first seven oracles. Then, in the case of the oracle against Israel, there are a total of ten offenses formally listed, but conceptually there are three (oppression, idolatry, corruption) and then a fourth (mistreatment of God's servants). Thus, Israel is the only offender for whom the list of offenses is completed with "three, even four." Israel is the true target of Amos's oracles all along. See Chisholm, "'For Three Sins . . . Even for Four,'" 188–97.

off the list, announces judgment, and then moves on to the next nation as if the real target of God's anger lies somewhere else. This stylistic device does not become a bad omen for Israel until the list of Judah's sins is [also] left truncated, suggesting that another nation, which proves to be Israel, will follow.[15]

As Amos's Israelite audience hears of the coming judgment on each of their surrounding antagonists, they would lean in closer to listen more carefully. They were sitting up, paying attention, receptive to what else Amos had to say, at least for the moment. Thus, Amos is demonstrating a brilliant introduction to his sermon, causing a hostile audience to want to lean in and listen, by using what some have called "a rhetoric of entrapment."[16] As Bullock notes, "once the auditors have been quite won over to the prophet's assessment of their neighbors, then Amos turns the tables and judges them according to the same standards. It was a trapdoor, and once inside, the door closed hopelessly behind them."[17] Chisholm summarizes Amos's technique: "a clear rhetorical pattern thus emerges in Amos 1–2. In the preliminary oracles the prophet gained his audience's attention and approval, leading them to believe that the Lord would soon intervene on their behalf and destroy the surrounding nations. When the prophet finally sprang his trap, he made it clear that Israel would be the primary object of the Lord's judgment because its guilt surpassed that of its neighbors."[18] Lessing playfully imagines the effect of a confrontational sermon thus introduced:

> From Amos 1:3 through 2:5 the prophet's audience, in all likelihood, cheered and applauded after each neighboring nation was condemned. "Great preacher, this Amos!" was the mantra of the moment. The sermon builds to a climax as three, four, and five nations are placed under divine fire. With the next judgment pointing to Judah (Amos 2:4–5), the number reaches seven. It was probably time for the Aaronic benediction (Num 6:22–27), a general dismissal, and then the normal post-service discussion about the weather and the events of the week. But Amos was not done preaching. The Lion was still roaring (cf. Amos 1:2; 3:8; 5:19). God's wrath was about to fall upon Israel.[19]

15. Chisholm, *Handbook on the Prophets*, 379.
16. Chisholm, "For Three Sins . . . Even for Four," 188.
17. Bullock, *An Introduction to the Old Testament Prophetic Books*, 78.
18. Chisholm, "For Three Sins . . . Even for Four," 190.
19. Lessing, *Prepare the Way of the Lord*, 472.

Part Two

Perhaps jubilant shouts of "Amen!" rose from the crowd. They liked what Amos had to say; they likely agreed that God's judgment for such offenses was right and well-deserved. When Amos's indictment focused on Judah, and lingered a little longer on the seventh of these nations, it likely seemed that the oracles were complete. Israel might even have been the most enthusiastic about God's judgment of Judah, against whom they harbored ongoing jealously and bitter rivalry. Israel's animosity against Judah had broken out in repeated wars, violence, and mistreatment against their own brothers, offenses which the preceding oracles had condemned. In condemning Judah and the others, they were also affirming God's condemnation of themselves.[20]

The Apostle Paul uses a similar tactic in the first two chapters of his epistle to the Romans. Romans 1:18–32 provides a graphic indictment against the ungodly who have denied their accountability to their creator. Their suppression of the truth of God culminates in obvious and heinous sin which we would expect the church in Rome to emphatically agree should be condemned. But Paul has a larger purpose than that. There is some subtle foreshadowing that his net is about to be cast more widely, when the seemingly worst of sinners are indicted together with their milder co-offenders: those "disobedient to parents, foolish, faithless" (1:30–31). When Romans chapter 2 opens, it becomes evident that the apostle's main purpose was not simply to condemn the ungodly, who deny any accountability to God. Paul, like Amos, is actually addressing an audience he surprises at the end of his indictment. His main audience all along is the religious person who judges others: "Therefore you have no excuse, O man, every one of you who judges. For in passing judgment on another you condemn yourself, because you, the judge, practice the very same things." (Rom 2:1). The "rhetoric of entrapment" which Nathan used on David and Amos used on Israel, Paul also used on religious people within the church.

Perhaps we might also employ this rhetoric of entrapment. For example, when preaching Romans 1:18–32 in a conservative church, it would be easy to focus mainly on the sins of those outside the church. However, we have not done justice to Paul's authorial intent if we don't let the sin we see in society serve as a bridge to confronting sin within the religious community.

20. Zephaniah similarly surprises his audience by turning judgment pronouncements against the surrounding nations back against Judah. The "oppressing city" (Zeph 3:1) might seem to still refer to Nineveh (2:13–15), but it soon becomes evident that the prophet is now referring again to Jerusalem (Zeph 3:2–5). See Chisholm, *Handbook on the Prophets*, 448, and Lessing, *Prepare the Way of the Lord*, 526.

For instance, while preaching on the topic of same-sex marriage not long ago, I had to take time to address the ways that Christians have, in practice, redefined marriage long before same-sex marriage ever became a societal possibility. When Christians have accepted and even participated in "no fault divorce" we have redefined that institution of which Jesus said, "What therefore God has joined together, let not man separate" (Matt 19:6). When we allow marriage to be about our own fulfillment and desires instead of "husbands, love your wives, as Christ loved the church and gave himself up for her" (Eph 5:25), we have redefined downward God's purpose for marriage. Amos's example showed me that while the topic of redefinition of marriage in society needed to be addressed, there was more that I needed to preach. Addressing the redefinition of marriage "out there" was important truth, but it also became the captivating introduction to confronting the redefinition of marriage within Christian circles.

READY TO HEAR

I owe a great debt to Donald Sunukjian for helping me to appreciate the importance of an engaging introduction when preaching. It is not that others had not impressed this upon me before, but Sunukjian explained it to me when I was ready to hear it—and that's just what a good introduction does, it gets the listener ready to hear. For too long, my interest in the Bible and its message hindered my preaching. I assumed that my listeners shared the same enthusiastic interest, or at least they would once I began showing them what was there. Since then I've learned that "the assumption that one's listeners automatically share one's own interest in the sermon is a mark of an inexperienced preacher."[21]

According to Sunukjian, the introduction of an expository sermon should engage the listeners, focus the message, and transition to the biblical passage. Of these three goals of the introduction, engaging the listeners is the longest and could take anywhere from two to ten minutes.[22] In the example of Amos's "for three sins and for four" introduction, the prophet

---

21. Chapell, *Christ-Centered Preaching*, 238.

22. Sunukjian, *Biblical Preaching*, 192–93. Balancing Sunukjian's (and Amos's) willingness to invest considerable time in the introduction, see Robinson, *Biblical Preaching*, 173. Robinson cautions that it should not be longer than needed, "once you get water, stop pumping"; don't be "so long spreading the table that [they lose their] appetite for the meal." Chapell, *Christ-Centered Preaching*, 239, suggests that listeners decide in the first 30 seconds whether they are interested in what the speaker has to say.

gives considerable time to arousing Israel's interest and agreement with his overarching precept before revealing his main point. If we were to take Amos 1–2 as its own sermon, the introduction is two-thirds of the entire sermon. Even if we were to read Amos 1–6 as one sermon, the introduction still comprises more than one-fifth of the entire message. In either case, the introduction is a very intentional and significant component in Amos's message and is essential to his sermon's persuasive effect. Whatever else we might learn from Amos, he made an intentional effort to engage his listeners. Sunukjian says "anything that engages the listeners and makes them want to hear the rest of the message is probably a good introduction."[23] Haddon Robinson says, "An introduction should command attention" and he supports this with a Russian proverb: "It is the same with men as with donkeys, whoever would hold them fast must get a good grip on their ears!"[24] In that case, Amos goes to the head of the class! He got a good grip on their ears! He had a message to proclaim which they would most likely stubbornly resist, so in his introduction he obtained their enthusiastic agreement with God's rationale for judgment before he ever applied that rationale to their own sin.

Now, I should not press this example of Amos too far. I cannot begin every sermon in this manner—they will be on to me in no time! If the introduction becomes too predictable, it could have the opposite effect: listeners may learn to pre-emptively put their defenses up or they may wander ahead, seeking to guess where I am going instead of listening. Sunukjian offers several different ways in which the preacher might engage his audience: relate an engaging personal story that draws them in, explore a contemporary issue (as in my marriage example, above), probe a common need, address a contradiction, offer to resolve some biblical difficulty, or make a startling statement.[25] We can find many of these same approaches used by the prophets.

Perhaps the best example of an engaging personal story that draws in the audience is the opening chapter of Hosea. Hosea's story also includes some biblical difficulties, because he is told by God to marry a wife who will

---

23. Sunukjian, *Biblical Preaching*, 193.

24. Robinson, *Biblical Preaching*, 166.

25. Sunukjian, *Biblical Preaching*, 193–99. Chapell, *Christ-Centered Preaching*, 246–48, has a similar list which includes: a human interest account, a simple assertion, a startling statement, a provocative question, an interesting quotation, or a catalog list of items, ideas or people.

be unfaithful to him.²⁶ This scandalous revelation immediately captures the audience and becomes a powerful metaphor for God's declaration against Israel (1:2–9). Hosea resolves some of the inherent tension of this personal story at the end of chapter one and in chapter three in order to illustrate Israel's future restoration. The prophet's return to the same image in his future oracles in chapters 4–9 helps make the abstract principle of spiritual unfaithfulness concrete and adds emotive persuasive force. These messages redacted together into the book of Hosea provide an excellent illustration of the power of continuing to use a central compelling image throughout the sermon.

The prophets also used contemporary issues to connect their message to their audience. Haggai explores whether it is really time to build the temple (Hag 1:2–4) and whether God was truly with them. These questions are directly related to the present lack of prosperity the returned exiles are experiencing. Joel uses a current locust plague (Joel 1:4) to foreshadow an even more terrible invading army which will stream down from the hills like locusts (2:2). Different expositors may differ on where the prophecy moves from locusts to armies, and what exact eschatological events are in view, but Joel's use of the current or previous locust plagues to anticipate a greater invader is clear. Seeing the prophet's use of contemporary events reminds us of two important principles to bring together in our sermons. We do well to speak to what people are already thinking about, but we should use what they are thinking about to help them see what they need to be thinking about: God's past redemption and future promise.²⁷

Isaiah, in his opening chapter, is probing a common need when he probes Israel's need for relief from God's chastening: "Your country lies desolate; your cities are burned with fire; in your very presence foreigners devour your land; it is desolate, as overthrown by foreigners. And the daughter of Zion is left like a booth in a vineyard, like a lodge in a cucumber field, like a besieged city" (Isa 1:7–8). This illustrates that contemporary issues lead to specific needs. Often times society's worst problems and most

---

26. It is not completely clear whether Hosea's wife, Gomer, was already a harlot before her marriage, or if Hosea is instructed to marry a woman who would later become a harlot. See Smith, *The Prophets as Preachers*, 72, and Chisholm, *Handbook on the Prophets*, 337.

27. Willhite, *Preaching with Relevance*, 87–88, points out that the felt needs which our congregations are thinking about are often "not necessarily the most significant questions that people need answered. Preachers need to "help listeners feel the need for the question(s)" which the text answers.

desperate needs point to issues of sin that must be confronted. Basic human needs, such as our need for companionship and relational connection, provide a bridge to a message about human relationship with the relational triune God.

Sometimes a message can be introduced by raising a difficulty or addressing a seeming contradiction. Habakkuk does this with great affect, when he, even though he is the prophet of God, dares to question what God is doing, or not doing (Hab 1:2–4). Habakkuk is actually probing the perplexing difficulty of theodicy, why a good and sovereign God allows evil to occur. The prophet poetically describes the breakdown of society and the rampant corruption and oppression after King Josiah's death.[28] By pointedly verbalizing the questions which are echoing in the hearts of his listeners, he also heightens his listeners' need for an answer—the questions can no longer be ignored. Habakkuk continues to use rhetorical questions to move his audience (and us) through his sermon toward the overarching principle, "the righteous shall live by his faith" (Hab 2:4). Then he shows the way to faith by remembering God's character (3:2) and his past redemptive faithfulness (3:3–15).

Finally, the prophets were also known for their startling statements. Malachi makes the startling statement from the Lord, "Oh that there were one among you who would shut the doors that you might not kindle fire on my altar in vain!" (Mal 1:10). To a people whose worship of the Lord revolved around the temple and the sacrifices there which God had required, this statement would seem to put the prophet in disagreement with Moses. It would certainly get their attention. Similarly, Zephaniah opens his prophecy by declaring that God will "utterly sweep away everything from the face of the earth" (1:2) Such a statement would seem contradictory to God's promise to Noah never again to destroy all living things from the earth (Gen 8:21). Can we effectively introduce a sermon by saying something that seems to contradict God's word?

Many years ago, after our first term of missionary service, I would often preach the Sunday sermon when we visited our supporting churches. Because the congregation was interested in our mission ministry, I normally began with some comments or stories relating to the work of our mission. I would describe how people had come to faith in Christ, and then

---

28. For a detailed and concise depiction of the historical background alluded to in Habakkuk, see Pinker, "Historical Allusions in the Book of Habakkuk," 143–52.

make the statement that "the goal of missions is not to see a lost person come to saving faith in Jesus Christ!"

Now, I'm not sure about your church, but in these churches that was a "startling statement," especially when coming from one of the church's missionaries! My preaching text for that message was Colossians 1:28–29, which begins: "Him [Jesus] we proclaim, warning everyone and teaching everyone with all wisdom, that we may present everyone mature in Christ." The text makes clear that the ultimate purpose or goal of Paul's missionary preaching was not the initial salvation of believers, but their continuing maturity in Christ. To put it another way, the great commission is to make disciples, not just converts.

Such a statement could have easily backfired and turned listeners away from listening. It would not have been helpful to extend that opening tension for very long without pointing toward some resolution. I would acknowledge the tension and clarify what I meant. "Seeing a lost soul come to faith in Jesus Christ" was not the goal, or end point in our mission. That was actually the first step toward an ultimate goal that our text (Col 1:28–29) would reveal. By suggesting that a long-cherished value of missionary evangelism was good, and yet still missing something, I had them waiting to hear what that something missing might be. They wanted to hear what I had to say. As Robinson says, we "must turn voluntary attention into involuntary attention, so that people listen not only because they ought to but because they want to."[29]

The faithful preaching pastor stands before the flock of God with the burden of the psalmist pressing on his heart: "Give ear, O my people, to my teaching; incline your ears to the words of my mouth" (Ps 78:1). May we learn from Amos and our preaching predecessors how our opening words might help the congregation to open their ears, so that we may rejoice together in "the glorious deeds of the Lord, and his might, and the wonders that he has done" (Ps 78:4).

---

29. Robinson, *Expository Preaching*, 161.

6

A Word Fitly Spoken

The Preacher sought to find delightful words
and to write words of truth correctly.
The words of wise men are like goads,
and masters of these collections are like well-driven nails.

ECCLESIASTES 12:10–11 NASB

The true rhetoric to which Paul adheres is the studied rhetoric of the sage who pores over ancient wisdom and turns of phrase, and who is renowned for instructive and persuasive speech.

JOHN LEVINSON[1]

The adage "Pray as if everything depended upon God and work as if everything depended upon you" can be applied to the preaching of God's word. Perhaps this is why the Apostles gave themselves "to prayer and to the ministry of the word" (Acts 6:4). They had to pray because they had to preach. The preacher is caught in what Azurdia calls "an occupational vulnerability" or an "inescapable frustration."[2] We are "possessed by a holy compulsion but hobbled by human inability."[3] This vulnerability or frustration is that the genuine spiritual effect of our preaching does not rest

---

1. Levison, "Did the Spirit Inspire Rhetoric," 40.
2. Azurdia, *Spirit Empowered Preaching*, 113.
3. Ibid., 125.

on our rhetorical efforts, and yet we devote ourselves to the rhetorical work of preparing sermons.

The Apostle Paul describes the tension between dependence on the Spirit's working and the significance of the preacher's rhetoric. He declares that his speech and "preaching were not in persuasive words of wisdom, but in demonstration of the Spirit and of power, that your faith should not rest on the wisdom of men, but on the power of God" (1 Cor 2:4 NASB). However, Paul gave particular attention to which words the Spirit would have him use: "we impart this in words not taught by human wisdom but taught by the Spirit" (1 Cor 2:13). Sunukjian summarizes: "In 1 Corinthians 2:1–5, therefore, Paul is not rejecting persuasion. Instead, he is recalling his continual determination to preach in a clear and cogent style, and to emphasize the message rather than the speaker."[4] The apostle did not *rely* on lofty speech or rhetoric to be persuasive, but he did use words well to speak persuasively. John Levison concludes that:

> Paul appears to disclaim rhetorical eloquence while at the same time writing with considerable rhetorical skill. This communicates that, although he appears to reject rhetoric, he is in fact a masterful proponent of rhetoric. The true rhetoric to which Paul adheres is the studied rhetoric of the sage who pores over ancient wisdom and turns of phrase, and who is renowned for instructive and persuasive speech.[5]

For too long in my preaching ministry I had such confidence that the Spirit would use God's word to convince the congregation that I gave insufficient attention to how I proclaimed God's word. I naively believed that if I was true to God's truth, the Spirit would do the rest.[6] I worked hard at biblical content, but neglected effective communication. I poured over the text to search out truth so that I could then inform others of the riches which were there. The problem is that to inform is not to persuade, and Paul shows us that Spirit-empowered preaching must have a biblical motive

---

4. Sunukjian, "The Preacher as Persuader," 296.

5. Levison, "Did the Spirit Inspire Rhetoric," 40.

6. One of the reasons conservative evangelicals are cautious of the notion of "prophetic preaching" is the inordinate emphasis some give to ecstatic utterance as prophecy. This overemphasis on ecstatic utterance has led some to neglect diligent study in favor of trusting the Spirit for the content of their preaching. Perhaps there is a similar error by biblical conservatives who would neglect rhetoric because we trust the Spirit for the effect of our preaching. We must do the diligent work of preparing our words for preaching even as we ask the Spirit to work through our preaching.

PART TWO

to persuade: "knowing the fear of the Lord, we persuade others" (2 Cor 5:11). Similarly, Luke summarizes Paul's evangelistic ministry as an effort to persuasion: "he reasoned in the synagogue every Sabbath, and tried to persuade Jews and Greeks (Acts 18:4). In the previous chapter we saw how the prophets got there audience to listen. In this chapter we will consider how the prophets sought to move their audience once they were listening.

PREACHING TO PERSUADE

We preach with the awareness that the call upon us to persuade men does not mean that the effectiveness of our ministry depends upon us rather than on the Spirit's working. Os Guinness warns:

> Christian persuasion must always know and show that the decisive power is not ours but God's. For God is his own lead counsel, his own best apologist, and the one who challenges the world to 'set out your case.' And as Jesus tells us, his Spirit, the Spirit of truth, is the one who does the essential work of convincing and convicting.[7]

Still, when God challenges the world to "set out your case," he does so through his messengers such as Isaiah (Isa 41:21; 43:26). The work of regeneration and salvation through faith is God's work, and yet God works through our words: "we are ambassadors for Christ, God making his appeal through us. We implore you on behalf of Christ . . . " (2 Cor 5:20). When we seek to implore and persuade, we should be aware of things God will use to help our words be persuasive.

Bryan Chapell provides a succinct summary of the three elements of classical persuasive rhetoric:

> In classical rhetoric, three elements compose every persuasive message:
>
> - *logos:* the verbal content of the message, including its craft and logic.
> - *pathos:* the emotive features of a message, including the passion, fervor, and feeling that a speaker conveys and the listeners experience.
> - *ethos:* the perceived character of the speaker, determined most significantly by the concern expressed for the listeners'

[7]. Guinness, *Fool's Talk*, 28.

welfare. Aristotle's belief (confirmed in countless modern studies) was that ethos is the most powerful component of persuasion.

> Listeners automatically evaluate each of these elements of persuasion in sermons in order to weigh the truths that the preacher presents. This realization should convince preachers who want to create clear access to the Word to strive to make each aspect of their messages a door and not a barrier.[8]

Each of these elements, logos, pathos, and ethos, can be discerned in the prophets' preaching long before Aristotle. There is always a *logos* or logic to their argument, "Come now, let us reason together, says the Lord" (Isa 1:18). The prophets are also very intentional about helping the audience feel persuasive emotional force, or *pathos*. One of the most common ways that the prophets evoked *ethos* was in declaring themselves to be sent from the Lord, while also showing concern for Israel. Many homiletics texts give attention to the *logos*, or reasoned argument of the sermon and the *ethos*, or personal integrity of the preacher, so it is unfortunate that most do not give the same attention to *pathos*, or emotional persuasion.[9] This is a critical issue, as Gitay points out, "The function of emotion in an argumentative discourse is important since it influences in a way which cannot be achieved by purely reasonable argument."[10]

For example, Warren Wiersbe describes the communicative difference between the two men who offer advice to Absalom immediately after he has deposed his father David in 2 Samuel 17.[11] First the respected advisor Ahithophel gives well-reasoned and concise logical counsel, anchored on his own authority as a wise advisor. His advice is good and is well-received, but it is not acted on. Competing advice is given by Hushai, the advisor David had left behind to misdirect Absalom's war council. While Ahithophel appealed to logic, Hushai paints a vivid picture using powerful emotional imagery; he shows what Absalom could do and how it would all look. He leads Absalom into imagining himself as the victorious general leading the armies of Israel and as a conquering king tearing down the walls of the city where David might hide. While Absalom heard and understood the logic of

---

8. Chapell, *Christ-Centered Preaching*, 34–35.

9. Two recent contributions which provide extensive discussions on emotional persuasion in preaching are Overstreet, *Persuasive Preaching*, and Guinness, *Fool's Talk*.

10. Gitay, "Reflections on the Study of the Prophetic Discourse," 218.

11. Wiersbe, *Preaching and Teaching with Imagination*, 15–16.

Ahithophel, he saw and felt the outcome depicted by Hushai. God used the emotionally persuasive counsel of Hushai to misdirect Absalom and save David. While the prophets also use reason and logic like Ahithophel, they skillfully present it with emotionally persuasive metaphors and images like Hushai. This effective use of emotional persuasion in preaching is one of the things today's preachers can learn from the prophets.

In the Spirit's divine working through men, which words we use and how we use them matter. This is evident in how we approach the Spirit-inspired text. We will carefully exegete the text of the apostle's epistle and the prophet's sermon, knowing that every word, as well as how the words are set together is vitally important. If speaking the right words in the right way was important in the sermons of the prophet's, who were "carried along by the Holy Spirit" (2 Pet 1:21), then the same should be true of our own preaching. We should give careful attention to words fitly spoken under the prayerful direction of the empowering Spirit, who has chosen to speak to men through men. This is why we prepare diligently and we pray desperately. This is why we study both hermeneutics and homiletics, in order that we might both exegete and exhort effectively.

Just as preachers benefit from the study of homiletics, rhetoric and communication theory, we also can benefit from considering what Spirit-empowered preaching has sounded like in the proclamation of our predecessors, the prophets. Rhetorical analysis of the sermons of the prophets, as found in the pages which follow, gives us that opportunity. It's something like being in a homiletics class and analyzing each of the students as they preach—only these sermons are better! When we pay attention to how the prophets say what God has given them to say, we can learn something about how to say what God has given us to say.

This is particularly true in our generation because the mindset of the prophets' audience toward their message was similar to our audience's mindset toward our message. The later prophets often preached among a society that had moved on from faith in the God of Israel to something else. Their audience knew something of God's covenant with Israel, but they had ceased to care. They held their heritage like the civil religion of twentieth-century America: a vague "In God we trust" sentimentality which denies any real power of God or accountability to God, whoever we might imagine God to be. Guinness describes the lack of interest in God's word today in terms reminiscent of the apparent disinterest in God's word when Isaiah stood before Ahaz (Isa 7). He says, "Most people quite simply are not open, not interested and not needy, and in much of the advanced modern world fewer people are open today than even a generation ago. Indeed, many are more hostile, and their hostility is greater than the Western church has faced for centuries."[12]

Even though their audience was often not eager to hear the word of the Lord, the prophets worked hard to be heard. They "spoke rhetorically and with an awareness of the effect their words would be likely to have on their immediate audience."[13] This is why Lessing encourages contemporary preachers to learn from the rhetorical devices, moves and strategies of the prophet's sermons. The Hebrew prophets effectively used "formulaic language, riddles, puns, sound-plays, rhetorical questions, and a definite rhythm in speech patterns . . . in order to aid in retention and persuasion."[14] Cultivating curiosity among a disinterested audience, reinforcing the retentive staying power of their message, and packing their preaching with emotional persuasion are three of the prophets' greatest strengths—strengths our preaching urgently needs. If we want people to continue listening beyond the introduction, to remember what we've said, and to be persuaded to act upon it, then we should learn from how the Spirit directed the preaching of the prophets.

Before we press further, I should mention an important limitation of this chapter and those that follow. It is not my goal to provide a list of stylistic devices which we should emulate. We will not see our preaching become more effective merely by mimicking the rhetorical techniques of the prophets. Guinness declares that "creative persuasion is a matter of truth, not simply of technique. More accurately, *creative persuasion is the art of truth, the art that truth inspires.*"[15] Guinness warns us against a tendency to "pursue the admirable goal of becoming more persuasive and to fall into a common trap: becoming preoccupied with technique, as if persuasion could be learned by observing the process carefully, reducing it to reason, reversing it and then repeating it ourselves."[16]

In the following pages, we will consider several sermons of the prophets and point out various rhetorical strategies that they employed. The goal is to demonstrate that the prophets were very intentional about using

---

12. Guinness, *Fool's Talk*, 22.
13. Barton, "Ethics in Isaiah of Jerusalem," 94.
14. Lessing, "Orality in the Prophets," 164. See also Boadt, "Prophetic Persuasion," 6.
15. Guinness, *Fool's Talk*, 34
16. Ibid., 35.

Part Two

rhetorical strategies and devices to increase the interest in, retention of and persuasion from their sermons. As we observe their preaching practice, it can provoke our own practice, not merely by mimicking them, but from reflectively considering how we might do the same kind of thing. As Kevin Miller says, "Although I can't just imitate great preachers, I can benefit greatly from their example."[17] The prophets can make us "more fully aware of the *whole* range of appeals embraced and provoked by rhetoric: not only the rational and cognitive dimensions, but also the emotive and imaginative ones."[18]

A CAREFULLY CRAFTED SERMON

One example of a prophet's sermon[19] which demonstrates exceptional rhetorical technique is Isaiah's parable of the vineyard and the following woe oracles (Isa 5:1–30), where the prophet "is at his rhetorical best."[20] Because a prophet's message and the rhetorical devices employed to communicate it are often linked to the historical setting,[21] it has been suggested that the sermon in Isaiah 5 is proclaimed during the Feast of Tabernacles.[22] The harvest is completed and there would be extensive partying in this week-long festival, to which Isaiah may allude (5:11–12, 22). It is also possible that there is a question hanging over the festivities: perhaps the harvest has not been good and the masses gathered are wondering what the cause might be. Maybe the later rains which normally would cause the land to flourish (Lev 26:4; Deut 28:12) did not come as needed (Isa 5:6b), leaving the fields and vineyards dry (Isa 5:24) and the grapes small and sour (Isa 5:4b). If that were the case, then Isaiah's sermon would resonate all the more with his

---

17. Miller, "Learning from the Giants," 711.

18. Wuellner, "Where is Rhetorical Criticism Taking Us," 461.

19. It is beyond the scope of this work to explore the historical critical issues involved in hypothesizing the original oral utterances of the prophets from later redactions. Renewed attention to literary redaction and orality studies in the last few decades have produced a significant body of literature which supports the conclusion that much more of the poetry and prose of the poetic books was the work of the preaching prophet and/or contemporary scribes. See Bullock, *An Introduction to the Old Testament Prophetic Books*, 38–42; Boadt, "Prophetic Persuasion," 1–21; Lessing, "Orality in the Prophets," 152–65; Wilson, "Current Issues in the Study of Old Testament Prophecy," 38–45.

20. Chisholm, *Handbook on the Prophets*, 22.

21. Boadt, "Prophetic Persuasion," 2.

22. Lessing, "Preaching Like the Prophets," 392.

audience. We should not make too much of a proposed historical setting and possible circumstances which the text is not explicit about, but the possibilities do suggest ways in which Isaiah may have chosen specific words and images to speak poetically and imaginatively to the situation at hand.

Isaiah's sermon occurs in three moves: the song of the vineyard (5:1–7), a funeral lament (5:8–25) and the concluding declaration of coming judgment (5:26–30).[23] Why does the prophet begin with a love song? A love song seems out of place when his main metaphor is a fruitless vineyard, the body of his message will be framed by oracles of doom, and his conclusion is the gloom of judgment. The simple answer is that he uses the opening love song to gain a hearing, to draw listeners in. The last thing the revelers at the feast want to hear is a prophetic judgment, no matter how poor the harvest may have been. This would be especially true among a generation that is not willing to hear God's word from his prophet (Isa 6:9–13). The love song is a means of gaining their attention and causing them to listen. As Isaiah, the friend of the bridegroom, takes up his song, perhaps the audience wonders if they know the bridegroom or his beloved. As the topic of the "love song" turns from the beloved to his vineyard, their curiosity is peaked even more. They likely wondered, "What is this poet talking about?"

The prophet employs a variety of rhetorical devices to make his message intriguing, captivating and memorable.[24] He wants it echoing in their memory long after the sermon is ended. He intentionally chooses words for similar sounding word plays and alliteration, although these techniques are often not evident in the English translation. He also employs poetic repetition of words and phrases such as "When I looked for it to yield grapes, why did it yield wild grapes?" (5:4).

Isaiah is also purposeful in his transitions: "*Now*" he draws his audience into his drama, and then invites them to form a judgment (5:3,4), "*And now* . . . what more was there to do?" Then he provides the answer in parallel terms, "*And now*, I will tell you what I will do" (5:5). When he sets the hook in verse 7, he does so with staccato parallelisms which are so well

23. Watts, *Isaiah 1–33*, 52–66. See also Chisholm, "Structure, Style and the Prophetic Message," 48, note 9. Chisholm points out that Isa 5:8–30 is structurally distinct from Isa 5:1–7. Still, the vine and wine imagery continues from the parable of the vineyard into the woe oracles (5:10–12, 22). This suggests that the parable of the vineyard serves as an introduction to the woe oracles and concluding judgment.

24. Lessing, "Preaching Like the Prophets," 392–94, provides an in-depth discussion of Isaiah's application of assonance, alliteration, paronomasia, inclusio, rhetorical questions and repetition based on the Hebrew text.

crafted they would not be easily forgotten: "He looked for justice (*mishpat*), but behold, bloodshed (*mispat*); for righteousness (*tsadaqah*), but behold, an outcry (*tse'aqah*)!" These wordplays poetically suggest that just as these words have been altered from good to evil, so also the audience has altered or perverted God's requirements.[25] Their behavior may have a veneer of acceptability, appearing to be good grapes, but they are in fact wild grapes and the Lord is not fooled by the resemblance.

Having grabbed their attention (and possibly having aroused an angry crowd), Isaiah uses a series of "woe oracles" to level his specific accusations that justice has been replaced by violence and righteousness has been replaced by the oppressed cries for relief. Isaiah's rhetorical artistry goes far beyond merely employing the woe oracle to evoke a mood of doom. Isaiah modifies the expected structure of the familiar form of these woe oracles somewhat and ties them together into a chiastic structure which provides a poetic repetition of the specific accusations the Lord has against them.[26] A woe oracle used in a judgment speech normally includes an accusation followed by an announcement of judgment. In Isaiah 5:8–30, there are six declarations of woe, but not all of the accusations are immediately followed with the announcement of judgment. Instead, the first accusation (5:8) is followed by a judgment as expected (5:9–10). Then two woe accusations are levelled (5:11–12), before their corresponding judgment is announced (5:13–17). Finally, four woe accusations are piled upon each other (5:18–23, 24b) before even greater judgments are declared (5:24a, 25–30).

This clustering of multiple accusations before the corresponding announcement judgment is a departure from the way the audience would expect the woe oracle to be used. Speaking in fresh unexpected ways is a strength of the prophets. Yehoshua Gitay has pointed out that the prophets could not be tied to the expected forms or stereotypical language in their speech, because "stereotypical language is the language of cliché . . . [and the] danger of cliché is the audience's passive response."[27] Similarly, Brueggemann explains why the prophets' revolutionary speech could not follow conventional forms:

> The shattering and forming of worlds is not done as a potter molds clay or as a factory makes products. It is done as a poet redescribes the world, reconfigures public perception, and causes people to

---

25. Chisholm, "Wordplay in the Eighth-Century Prophets," 49.
26. Chisholm, "Structure, Style, and the Prophetic Message," 49–53.
27. Gitay, "Reflections on the Study of the Prophetic Discourse," 213.

re-experience their experience. To do that requires that speech must not be conventional, reasonable or predictable: it must shock sensitivity, call attention to what is not noticed, break the routine, cause people to redescribe things that have long since seem settled.[28]

Thus, the prophet departs from the expected conventional form of the woe oracle in order to effectively convey unexpected and unconventional realities.[29] Isaiah's example suggests to us that it can be important to use common language in uncommon, unexpected ways, in order to be heard. For example, some time ago a well-known personality was in the news for trans-gender surgery. It was expected that I speak against this practice, and say many of the same things people were already saying among themselves or had heard someone else say. Instead, I chose to talk about a recent phenomenon called "trans-abled." This unconventional term describes a person who mentally does not feel right with a "whole" physical body and identify themselves with some physical disability. They seek to surgically acquire a disability of one kind or another, such as blindness or even limb amputation. Such extremely bizarre dysfunction made the point that mental confusion about one's physical body should be helped mentally, not acquiesced to by physical surgery. I spoke to what needed to be addressed, but by doing so in an unexpected way I helped the issues be considered on a deeper level.

Isaiah has unexpectedly departed from the expected form of the woe oracle, clustering these accusations together. The battering effect of the clustering of accusations in Isaiah 5:8–23, especially in verses 18–23, suggests that Isaiah's sermon is intended to have an emotional as well as a rational effect. The prophet is not only trying to cognitively convince them, he also seeks to emotionally persuade. The prophet's use of poetry and poetic prose is far more emotionally persuasive than logical prose would be, just as teaching is not as exhortationally effective as preaching. As Lessing says, the prophetic "texts are literary artistries . . . engaging the audience in an emotional dialogue, in contrast to teaching, which is logical and rational."[30] Good preaching conveys emotion, not just information.

28. Brueggemann, "The Book of Jeremiah," 138.

29. Following this sermon, Isaiah will also apply the same woe form to himself, identifying himself with the sinful nation, "Woe is me! For I am lost; for I am a man of unclean lips, and I dwell in the midst of a people of unclean lips" (Isa 6:5). But that use, while instructive of the humility of the preacher, is not a component of this sermon.

30. Lessing, "Preaching Like the Prophets," 402, 405.

Finally, this clustering of woes also ties the various accusations together into a unified whole which describes Israel's complete and total disregard of God and his covenant, leaving no option except judgment. This is where the sermon concludes with its most picturesque imagery of all. An invading nation will be summoned whose mighty men are not "heroes at drinking wine" (cp. Isa 5:22), but are disciplined and ready warriors, fierce as lions, as unstoppable as the sea. In sharp contrast to the opening pastoral image of a fertile vineyard on the hill, they now behold the gathering storm of a looming invasion and there is no escape. The joy of the harvest celebration has been replaced by darkness and distress. John Broadus has advised preachers that, "A message that starts with a gripping introduction should end with an even more powerful conclusion."[31] Isaiah's sermon has done just that. He grips his audience in the midst of their post-harvest revelry. His creative use of imagery and forms keeps his audience with him. His emotionally persuasive rhetoric impresses the enormity of the situation upon them. His dramatic conclusion undoubtedly has deflated the prevalent party atmosphere. Whether or not they have received it, God's word has been heard.

It is clear that Isaiah has done more than simply declare Israel's guilt and predict coming judgment. God's messenger has carefully constructed an imaginatively memorable and emotionally persuasive sermon. What is even more remarkable is that this outstanding example of sermonic composition immediately precedes a declaration from the Lord that Isaiah is to proclaim God's message even though his audience will not listen (Isa 6:9–13). This suggests that our purpose in giving careful attention to how we preach is not merely to ensure results. We give careful attention to how we proclaim God's word in order to rightly honor God's word. We seek to declare it well because it is the word of God and so it should be declared well. Even if it is true that many will not listen, it must never be because we are hard to listen to.

The prophets' sermons were easy to listen to. Intriguing imagery draws the audience in. Unexpected twists and turns keep them listening, just as plot twists hold a contemporary audience through a typical television drama. The prophets used unexpected rhetorical twists "to arouse emotional excitement, surprise and avoid monotony" so that the audience is not passive but become active participants.[32] The creative use of assimila-

---

31. Broadus, *On the Preparation and Delivery of Sermons*, 123.
32. Gitay, "Deutero-Isaiah: Oral or Written," 195.

tion, mnemonics and wordplays helps their message to linger long after the sermon is ended.

THE PUNNING PROPHET

Another example of how the prophets used wordplays to give their sermons longer life is their use of puns or paronomasias, words that sound the same. For example, Micah has an extended series of puns or wordplays based on the locations mentioned in Micah 1:10–15. "The lament is largely a series of puns on the names of twelve cities. The names of twelve cities in the Shephelah are given meaning symbolic of the judgment which God was bringing on them in the form of an invader, probably the king of Assyria."[33] These puns are easy to overlook in the English versions, but obvious in Hebrew. To reveal Micah's puns, I'll quote the English text, with the Hebrew meanings of the locations included in brackets (an asterisk indicates that the location name sounds like a word with the meaning provided in brackets):

>Tell it not in Gath;
>>weep not at all;
>
>in Beth-le-aphrah [house of dust]
>>roll yourselves in the dust.
>
>Pass on your way,
>>inhabitants of Shaphir [beautiful],
>>in nakedness and shame;
>
>the inhabitants of Zaanan [one who comes out to battle]
>>do not come out;
>
>the lamentation of Beth-ezel [house that stands by another]
>>shall take away from you its standing place.
>
>For the inhabitants of Maroth [bitterness*]
>>wait anxiously for good,
>
>because disaster has come down from the Lord
>>to the gate of Jerusalem.
>
>Harness the steeds to the chariots,
>>inhabitants of Lachish [steeds*];
>
>it was the beginning of sin
>>to the daughter of Zion,

---

33. Smith, *Micah-Malachi*, 20. See also Chisholm, *Handbook on the Prophets*, 418–19.

Part Two

> for in you were found
>> the transgressions of Israel.
> Therefore you shall give parting gifts
>> to Moresheth-gath [dowry gift*];
> the houses of Achzib [lie*] shall be a deceitful thing
>> to the kings of Israel.
> I will again bring a conqueror to you,
>> inhabitants of Mareshah [conqueror*];
> the glory of Israel
>> shall come to Adullam.

To summarize Micah's *punnish* preaching: the house of dust will roll in dust, the beautiful will be shamed, those who go out will not go out, the one who stands by another will be taken away, and those who seek good will find bitterness. The city of chariots will ready her chariots to no avail, those with dowry gifts will themselves be given away, the deceitful will be deceived, and the conquerors of the poor will themselves be conquered. The effect of Micah's word play would be especially impactful on those who lived in any of these locations. He has given new meanings to common names, so that his audience will be reminded of his message whenever one of these locations is brought to mind.

There is one more bit of poetic irony, hidden a little below the surface for those paying closer attention. The cities with which Micah opens and closes, Gath and Adullam, have no word play associated with them. They are conspicuous by the absence of a pun. Instead, they each evoke an episode in the life of David. "Tell it not in Gath . . . " is a quote from David's lament upon learning of the death of Saul and Jonathan (2 Sam 1:20). There David lamented that "the glory of Israel had been slain" (2 Sam 1:19). Here, Micah declares that "the glory of Israel will come to Adullum" again, like it had when David fled to Adullam from Gath while he was pursued by Saul (1 Sam 22:1). These two references serve as a multi-faceted inclusio: they remind of a previous time when Israel's leadership (Saul) had departed from God, and God's judgment came by defeat at the hands of Israel's enemies. And yet, there is also a hint of hope: Saul was defeated, but David would then reign. The reference to Adullum could remind them that even though David went through a time of fleeing from enemies on every side, still God preserved him and restored him.

Micah has used puns to help his message to be retained in the memory of his audience. Because it is retained, they would have opportunity to reflect more on the ironic justice of God, as well as the deeper aspects of hope and restoration which can follow judgment. Reminded by the puns and reflecting on the allusions marked out by a lack of puns, the audience has a greater opportunity to hear Micah's warning and respond rightly to it.

Other prophets also used word plays, or as Gitay says, their "oral presentation utilized sound effects." He shows that sound plays and repetitions dominate Isaiah 40:1–11 and suggests they attract attention and make the message more aesthetically pleasing to hear.[34] Nahum ironically strings three words of judgment together in memorably alliterated assonance, "*buqah, umebuqah, umebulaqah*," which is translated as "Destruction, devastation and desolation" (Nah 2:10 NET). A similar pair of alliterated assonance in Hebrew occurs in Lamentations 3:48, which is also nicely recreated in English, "panic and pitfall have come upon us, devastation and destruction" (Lam 3:47). The prophets have given intentional effort to proclaim God's truth in emotionally impactful ways. Preachers today must do the same.

CONVINCING A RELUCTANT AUDIENCE

One of the difficult realities of preaching is that we are called to persuade a reluctant audience of truth they would rather avoid but need to believe. The persuasive sermon in Amos chapters 3–4 is another example of a prophet's sermon using a variety of rhetorical devices and literary forms to draw the audience toward a conclusion they would rather avoid. In the past, excessive fixation on forms has led scholars to shatter Amos chapter three into many broken pieces. However, Gitay has shown that Amos intentionally combined these various devices into a unified and effective rhetorical whole,[35] which likely continues into chapter four.[36] In this sermon, we can hear Amos combine several different forms of appeal together for a greater persuasive effect.

Amos begins by making a logical appeal for the relationship between cause and effect, in order to convince his audience that their sin must cause or result in a divinely appointed catastrophic judgment. He does this by using multiple analogies (3:3–6a) which would be near to the audience's

---

34. Gitay, "Deutero-Isaiah: Oral or Written," 195–96.

35. Gitay, "A Study of Amos's Art of Speech," 294–96.

36. Stuart, *Hosea-Jonah*, 328, shows that the message of Amos 3 most likely continues into Amos 4.

own experiences and which lead to an obvious conclusion: God will bring judgment upon them through a catastrophic crisis (3:6b).

> 3 "Do two walk together,
> unless they have agreed to meet?
> 4 Does a lion roar in the forest,
> when he has no prey?
> Does a young lion cry out from his den,
> if he has taken nothing?
> 5 Does a bird fall in a snare on the earth,
> when there is no trap for it?
> Does a snare spring up from the ground,
> when it has taken nothing?
> 6 Is a trumpet blown in a city,
> and the people are not afraid?
> Does disaster come to a city,
> unless the Lord has done it? (Amos 3:3–6).

Following this bold declaration, Amos softens his tone somewhat with an ethical appeal, demonstrating an apologetic stance similar to, "I'm sorry, but I have to tell you this . . ." Gitay suggests that Amos's purpose in Amos 3:7–8 is to demonstrate that he has appropriate empathy toward his audience, as well as credibility as God's prophet.[37]

> 7 "For the Lord God does nothing
> without revealing his secret
> to his servants the prophets.
> 8 The lion has roared;
> who will not fear?
> The Lord God has spoken;
> who can but prophesy?" (Amos 3:7–8).

Next, the weight of additional witnesses, or a comparison to a recognized evil, is added by the rhetorical summoning of heathen nations to confirm Israel's sin. Finally, the prophet will appeal to their past experience of already experiencing God's judgments (4:6–11). In this case, God's "past performance does guarantee future results." This section is unified by the repeated refrain, "yet you did not return to me," which here serves

---

37. Gitay, "Amos's Art of Speech," 299. See also Stuart, *Hosea-Jonah*, 325–26.

as an implied invitation to repentance as well as justification for coming judgment.

> 6 "I gave you cleanness of teeth in all your cities,
>   and lack of bread in all your places,
>   yet you did not return to me,"
>   declares the Lord.
> 7 "I also withheld the rain from you
>   when there were yet three months to the harvest;
>   I would send rain on one city,
>   and send no rain on another city;
>   one field would have rain,
>   and the field on which it did not rain would wither;
> 8 so two or three cities would wander to another city
>   to drink water, and would not be satisfied;
>   yet you did not return to me,"
>   declares the Lord.
> 9 "I struck you with blight and mildew;
>   your many gardens and your vineyards,
>   your fig trees and your olive trees the locust devoured;
>   yet you did not return to me,"
>   declares the Lord.
> 10 "I sent among you a pestilence after the manner of Egypt;
>   I killed your young men with the sword,
>   and carried away your horses,
>   and I made the stench of your camp go up into your nostrils;
>   yet you did not return to me,"
>   declares the Lord.
> 11 "I overthrew some of you,
>   as when God overthrew Sodom and Gomorrah,
>   and you were as a brand plucked out of the burning;
>   yet *you did not return to me*,"
>   declares the Lord (Amos 4:6–11, emphasis added).

Amos has applied something similar to what Sunukjian calls "the developmental questions" of sermon development, which include "What do

I need to explain," "Do we buy it," and "What does it look like in real life?"[38] Amos first addressed the belief question, "Do we believe God will judge us?" with appeals to reason, witnesses and experience as described above. He also saw the need to "explain" his own prophetic stance, to prevent personal feelings against the messenger from obscuring the message. Finally, he concludes the sermon by giving a specific description of what God's judgment has looked like (4:6–11) and will look like (4:12–13). While the developmental question "What does it look like in real life?" is often used for concrete examples of positive application, it can also be used, as here, to provide specific examples of what the consequences will look like in real life to emphasize the need for repentance.

Amos's use of vivid imagery and metaphors add an emotional dimension which increases persuasiveness. The lion roaring is the voice of God which cannot be ignored (3:8). The metaphor of the shepherd who can only rescue bits and pieces of the lamb devoured by a lion (3:12) may have been especially emotional for Amos, a shepherd (1:1), to convey. Thus it would have also been more emotionally persuasive for his audience to hear. In this sermon Amos has applied the *logos* (rational), *ethos* (character), and *pathos* (emotional) elements described by Chapell as critical for effective persuasion.

The sermon's overall structure has also been carefully constructed. The sermon opens and closes with a declaration of God's transcendent sovereignty, as the basis for God's call and Israel's accountability (3:1–2; 4:12–13). Next are the persuasive appeals of reason (3:3–12) and experience (4:6–11). Finally, the cause of judgment is brought into clearer focus at the center of the sermon (3:13—4:5). The idolatrous worship at Bethel (3:14; 4:4) bookends a central indictment of their pride which leads them to oppress others in servitude (4:1). Even the shifting of forms within these two chapters, which often led scholars to fragment them into separate utterances daisy-chained together, has a rhetorical purpose: holding his audience's interest. Through the moves of his message, Amos has used various forms in unexpected ways to "attract attention, create curiosity, and enable the speaker to convey the message effectively."[39]

A contemporary example of the effectiveness of a shift in form could occur at a wedding, which may be one of the hardest places for a sermon to truly be heard due to the ready distractions and one's expectation that they already know generally what the preacher is going to say. The expected,

---

38. Sunukjian, *Biblical Preaching*, 87.
39. Gitay, "Amos's Art of Speech," 306.

familiar form would be something like: "We are gathered together here today to unite these two. . . . " But, what if the pastor were to begin his remarks with a series of questions: "Why are we gathered together here today? For what reason have we come to witness these vows? What is this thing called holy matrimony?" This unexpected shift would likely arouse interest in the central point the preacher will speak to, whereas the expected form is more likely to invite the audience to mentally wander off while the pastor "does his preaching bit." Questions have a way of drawing in the audience.

PUTTING THE QUESTION TO THEM

Amos's sermon provides a good example of the effective use of rhetorical questions to draw the audience into the preacher's line of thought. There are seven rhetorical questions in Amos 3:3–6. The series of questions begins seemingly innocuously, "Can two walk together unless they have agreed to meet?" Next, the questions affirm norms of nature, although with a somewhat calamitous edge in their imagery of prey being taken, and snares entrapping. Then, the final two questions suggest a cry of alarm and disaster befalling a city. Through this series of questions, the preacher has provided a preparatory path for his audience to be more willing to respond to a warning of danger. Then, after a brief explanatory pause (3:7), an eighth rhetorical question reveals his true point: God's prophetic warning must be feared and the prophet has no choice but to declare it (3:8).[40]

The prophet Jeremiah also effectively uses rhetorical questions in multiple ways. Like the examples in Amos, Jeremiah uses questions concerning their common knowledge of nature to lead his audience to affirm a conclusion which they are reluctant to admit. The compatibility of flints to a field, snow to Lebanon and flowing streams to bubbling springs are used to contrast the incompatibility of God's people and idols (Jer 18:14–15). Jeremiah frequently uses pairs of rhetorical questions to affirm generally accepted positive presuppositions (Jer 2:14; 2:31–32; 3:1–5; 8:4). In these examples, the initial questions are then contrasted to present conditions which beg a different question. "In each case the question is turned to show that Israel

---

40. Möller, *A Prophet in Debate:*, 225–28. Möller also points out that Amos's seven initial questions which get closer and closer to the point and then lead into a climactic eighth question, is a repeat of the 7+1 strategy employed in Amos 1–2. This climactic eighth question, which is expressed as a parallel couplet for emphasis, is the main point he has been leading his audience to accept.

has acted in unnatural and unexpected ways." Brueggemann explains that Jeremiah uses accepted truth about God to force the audience to question why their present experience doesn't agree with these presuppositions (Jer 8:19; 8:22).[41]

One of the best known rhetorical questions found in the prophets was asked by God of Ezekiel, "Son of man, can these bones live?" (Ezek 37:3). Here the obvious answer from natural experience would be "No." However, in this case the question is posed to plant hope when there is no normal expectation of hope or restoration. The question implies that God will do what they do not expect he would do. The rhetorical question is part of an elaborate staging of the point, which makes the promised resurrection all the more memorable.[42] The prophet is then told to prophesy over the bones, that God might make them live. This underscores an important aside: when God miraculously brings life out of death, he does so through the preaching of his messengers. Yet again we are reminded that for anything to change, God must work, but God chooses to work through those whom he sends to preach his word.

Why do the prophets make such extensive use of rhetorical questions? Why is "Can these bones live" the line we most easily remember from the book of Ezekiel? Os Guinness explains why questions are effective when addressing an audience that is not inclined to agree with the speaker:

> Questions are always more subversive than statements. For one thing, they are indirect. Whereas it should be crystal clear what a statement is saying and where it is leading, a good question is not so obvious, and where it leads to is hidden. For another thing, questions are involving. Whereas a statement always has a "take it or leave it" quality, and we may or may not be interested in what it tells us, there is no standing back from a well-asked question. It invites us, challenges us or intrigues us to get into it and follow it to see where it leads. In short, even a simple question can be a soft form of subversion.[43]

Guinness insists that this "subversive" use of questions is even more critical in an era when our audience is more inclined to decide matters of faith on their own opinion rather than from some spiritual authority.

---

41. Brueggemann, "Jeremiah's Use of Rhetorical Questions," 360–63.
42. Fox, "The Rhetoric of Ezekiel's Vision of the Valley of the Bones," 10–11.
43. Guinness, *Fool's Talk*, 52.

Speaking of an age in which the population defers to experts in almost every area of life except matters of faith, he writes:

> Everyone is naturally convinced that their own faith is adequate and true, and almost as naturally convinced that what others believe simply cannot be true, whether they are honest or rude enough to say so. That is even more the case with the mind and heart that is firmly closed—but this is precisely where questions come in. The person who will not listen to anyone from the outside who raises anything against his or her faith is still always open to the power of questioning.[44]

Thus, as Gitay says, when the audience is addressed with rhetorical questions, they are forced "to respond and thus to take an active role in the persuasion process."[45] C. J. Labuschagne concurs: "The rhetorical question is one of the most forceful and effective ways employed in speech for driving home some idea or conviction. Because of its impressive and persuasive effect the hearer is not merely a listener: he is forced to frame the expected answer in his mind and, and by doing so he actually becomes the co-expresser of the speaker's conviction."[46] Rhetorical questions "induce the addressee to mentally agree that the implied assertion is true. The rhetorical question ... exerts psychological pressure upon the addressee by implying that any reasonable person would agree with the implied assertion."[47] Therefore, we should learn from the prophets' use of rhetorical questions in order to better persuade contemporary audiences which have become hardened to the gospel.

SPRING-LOADED SERMONS

This survey of just a few of the prophets' sermons has demonstrated that the prophets, under the inspiration of the Spirit, were intentional about how they used words to proclaim God's word. Their messages were carefully crafted to persuasively engage an audience which was often not favorably disposed to their message. They did not rely upon rhetoric for results, but they did apply rhetoric effectively for the results which God might mercifully grant. In an age when words had become misused by false prophets,

44. Ibid., 162.
45. Gitay, "Deutero-Isaiah," 197.
46. Labuschagne, *The Incomparability of Yahweh in the Old Testament*, 23.
47. Moshavi, "What Can I Say," 97.

Part Two

God still chose to use the foolishness of preaching, empowered by his Spirit and "spring-loaded" with persuasive effect,[48] to accomplish his purpose and declare his glory.

We preach in an era which has some similarity to the era in which the prophets preached. The gospel, or what people assume the gospel to be, is not heard as a new and revolutionary message as it was in the first century. Instead, the gospel is perceived much as later Israel perceived the covenantal message of the prophets: "That Yahwehism is so 1400s, does anyone really still believe that?" It is heard as a familiar but outdated message from which people believe they have already moved on. They assume they have already heard, and rejected, the message we preach, even though they may have actually rejected a poor caricature of the real gospel. Thus we need to work as hard as the prophets worked, to speak as well as the prophets spoke, to give our listeners the best opportunity to hear. This is not because they deserve it, but because the gospel deserves it. Thus Guinness concludes:

> All such ways of spring-loading our persuasion are vital today, for words themselves are at a historic low point in the advanced modern world. On the one hand, modern words suffer from inattention. Everyone is speaking and no one is listening. On the other hand, modern words suffer from inflation. Under the impact of the omnipresence of advertising and "adspeak" words are nothing more than tools to sell products and agendas, and the highest and most sacred words can be used to give a leg up to the most trivial of goods and the worst of causes. Words today are all so much "verbiage," "propaganda" and a matter of "words, words, words."
>
> In direct and forceful contrast, we Christians must show again that we are both people of the Word and people who believe in words. Words are never mere words for us, for they are linked indissolubly to truth, freedom, worship and human dignity. Words matter because we worship the Word himself, and our words used on his behalf should be spring-loaded with the truth and power of his Word—especially to those who are closed.[49]

Another well-known preacher also served in a generation when words about God needed to gain a new hearing. Concerning preachers of the gospel, Martin Luther said:

---

48. Guinness, *Fool's Talk*, 72–73 and 149–67, uses the image of a spring-loaded mousetrap to describe the turning of tables from one's carefully constructed alternate reality to the sudden realization of how things really are.

49. Ibid., 166–67

> Certainly it is my desire that there shall be as many poets and rhetoricians as possible, because I see that by these studies, as by no other means, people are wonderfully fitted for the grasping of sacred truth and for handling it skillfully and happily. Therefore I beg of you that at my request (if that has any weight) you will urge your young people to be diligent in the study of poetry and rhetoric.[50]

At a time when the gospel urgently needed a fresh hearing, Luther urged preachers to give artful attention to how they proclaimed it. In such a hostile environment for God's word, the work of preaching would be a futile effort if the Living God were not in it. But God is working; God is revealing himself through words. Therefore, like the prophets before us, we must prayerfully and intentionally use our words to preach his word.

---

50. Smith and Jacobs, *Luther's Correspondence and Other Contemporary Letters*, 2:176–77.

7

Let Me Be Clear

It is not enough to know what we ought to say; we must also say it as we ought ...the way in which a thing is said does affect its intelligibility.

ARISTOTLE[1]

...pray also for us, that God may open to us a door for the word, to declare the mystery of Christ, on account of which I am in prison—that I may make it clear, which is how I ought to speak.

COLOSSIANS 4:3–4

If the Old Testament prophets are examples from whom preachers should learn, and one of the essentials of good preaching is oral clarity, this seems to pose a problem. It seems somewhat presumptuous to approach the prophets as exemplars of clarity in their sermons, since their message is often hard for us to understand. As one Old Testament scholar notes:

> The prophetic literature of the Hebrew Bible presents great interpretive obstacles. Its poetry, though teeming with vivid imagery that engages the imagination and emotions, challenges the reader's understanding because of its economy of expression, rapid shifts in mood, and sometimes cryptic allusions. The reader of the prophetic literature quickly realizes that these books were written at

---

1. Aristotle, *Rhetoric,* 120–21.

particular points in time to specific groups of people with whom the modern reader seems to share little.[2]

Of course, as Chisholm recognizes, the fact that cultural and chronological distance contribute to our difficulty in understanding conversely suggests that these obstacles would not have been present for the original audience. This ancient Hebrew poetry, which gives us interpretive challenges, would have conveyed depth of meaning and emotion in an economy of words with the same clarity as a well-known popular song does today. For instance, the refrain to Harry Chapin's classic song, "Cat's in the Cradle" evokes stirring memories and emotions of family dysfunction and a father's lack of connection that repeats itself in the next generation. That's a lot to pack into a few lines of poetry!

In the same way, the prophets conveyed significant and powerful meaning in an economy of words. Because of the cultural and chronological distance between us and ancient Israel, we have difficulty in understanding, but that's a difficulty which the original hearers of the prophet's messages did not have. To their original audiences, we can assume that the prophets were very clear. The complaint against the prophets in their time was not that they were not understood, but that their audience did not like what they understood the prophets to say (cf. 1 Kgs 22:8–18; Amos 7:1–13; Jer 26:1–11). In fact, the prophets employed many of the same rhetorical strategies for oral clarity which students of preaching are urged to employ today.

Donald Sunukjian, in *Invitation to Biblical Preaching: Proclaiming Truth with Clarity and Relevance*, demonstrates that oral messages lack several advantages for clarity which are inherent to written communication, and so oral clarity must be intentionally enhanced. Sunukjian prescribes six principles which preachers should use to enhance the oral clarity of their message.[3] Four of these six are clearly observable in the prophets:

1. Restate critical (important) sentences, saying the same thing in different words.

2. Consistently use the same key language or phrasing.

3. Use rhetorical questions to transition from one major movement to the next.

4. Present each new main point in a deductive manner.

---

2. Chisholm, *Handbook on the Prophets*, 9.
3. Sunukjian, *Introduction to Biblical Preaching*, 268–94.

Part Two

In the following pages we will see how Sunukjian's principles for oral clarity are also evident in the first recorded sermon of Jeremiah. In the opening chapter of the book of Jeremiah, the prophet is introduced and his prophetic call from the Lord is described (Jer 1:1–19). The prophet's ministry of judgment upon Judah's idolatry is summarized, along with the nation's unbending rebellious response. Following this call narrative, we come to Jeremiah's first sermon (Jer 2:1—3:5), which is a persuasive summary of the Lord's quarrel with his people. In this sermon the prophet employs multiple rhetorical strategies which enhance the clarity of his message. For example, Jeremiah often restates, his key indictments, or as Sunukjian says, he restates critical sentences.

RESTATE CRITICAL SENTENCES

Restatement does not mean to say the same thing again, by simply repeating the same words. Restatement is saying the same thing again but with different words. This allows a second chance to hear that critical sentence if a listener had become distracted. Saying the same thing again with different words also allows another chance to understand, if the wording used the first time was unclear to a listener. The poetry of the prophets relies heavily upon restatement.

For example, Jeremiah restates his initial charge against Judah in multiple parallel phrases. Jeremiah asks "What wrong did your fathers find in me that they went far from me, and went after worthlessness, and became worthless? They did not say, 'Where is the Lord who brought us up from the land of Egypt . . . ?" (Jer 2:5–6.) The fault of going far from the Lord is restated as going after worthlessness (idolatry), which is again restated as not calling on the Lord who had redeemed them from Egypt. The fact that the worthlessness refers to idolatry is verified by the similar restatements in Jer 2:8: "The priests did not say, 'Where is the Lord?' Those who handle the law did not know me; the shepherds transgressed against me; the prophets prophesied by Baal and went after things that do not profit." The people not calling on the Lord (2:8a) is possibly restated as "not knowing me" and "transgressed against me" and is contrastingly stated as prophesying by Baal and going after "things that do not profit."

In the next section of his sermon, Jeremiah declares that they are enduring the consequences of covenant unfaithfulness as predicted in

Deuteronomy 28. The prophet implies this by restating in several ways the same general catastrophes they are facing:

> The lions have roared against him; they have roared loudly.
> They have made his land a waste; his cities are in ruins, without inhabitant.
> Moreover, the men of Memphis and Tahpanhes have shaved the crown of your head.
> Have you not brought this upon yourself by forsaking the LORD your God, when he led you in the way? (Jer 2:15–17)

The lions that have roared refer to an invasion, likely Assyria, not wild beasts.[4] Invaders have laid to waste their land and cities. Adding further clarity, there have been multiple invasions because there are multiple invaders, as they have also been abused by Egypt (Memphis and Tahpanhes).

A third example of parallel restatement is found in a further condemnation of Judah's idolatry in Jeremiah 2:26–28:

> As a thief is shamed when caught, so the house of Israel shall be shamed:
> they, their kings, their officials, their priests, and their prophets,
> who say *to a tree*, 'You are my father,'
> and *to a stone*, 'You gave me birth.'
> For they have turned their back to me, and not their face.
> But in the time of their trouble they say, 'Arise and save us!'
> But where are your gods that you made for yourself?
> Let them arise, if they can save you, in your time of trouble;
> for as many as your cities are your gods, O Judah. (Emphasis mine.)

They have turned to idols of wood and stone, that is, they have turned away from the Lord; they have made gods for themselves.

A specialized form of repetition or restatement is accumulation, the piling up of descriptive terms, one upon another. Accumulation is abundant in Jeremiah, "with nouns heaping up in twos, threes, and fours, and longer phrases balancing rhythmically in parallelism."[5] An example of accumulation occurs in Jeremiah 2:6, "... who led us in the wilderness, in a land of deserts and pits, in a land of drought and deep darkness." While this is not exactly the same as Sunukjian's principle of restatement, the accumulation of parallel terms paints a more vivid image of the type of experience through which the Lord had led his people. Gitay explains that

---

4. Chisholm, *Handbook on the Prophets*, 156.
5. Lundbom, *The Hebrew Prophets*, 179.

in their elaboration by repetition, the speech dwells more vividly on the subject, which "stirs emotions and evokes responses that involve the audience" more intensively in the message.[6]

Thus, in Jeremiah 2:26 the prophet could have simply said "all the people" or "the people and the leaders." But, using accumulation to say "they, their kings, their officials, their priests, and their prophets" is more striking. This use of accumulation also gets our attention because the order of the list from kings to prophets might be related to the level of authority persons have in society, except that "they," the common people, are listed first. Because he expanded on that point, the audience may have concluded Jeremiah is saying more than merely that all the leaders are corrupt. Perhaps the prophet is also subtly implying that the spiritual downfall of Israel is not merely the result of wicked kings, but the actions of each and every person, all the house of Israel. This is another example where paying attention to how the prophet says what he says can also enrich our understanding of his message.

It could be argued that what I am calling restatement which enhances clarity is really only the parallelism common to Hebrew poetry. I will concede that point if it is also agreed that these parallel restatements are partly what gave such powerful clarity to Hebrew poetry.[7] I am not trying to demonstrate that the prophets employed our contemporary homiletical strategies on our terms. Rather, I am asserting that rhetorical techniques similar to current techniques—which we believe enhance preaching—are also effectively demonstrated by the Hebrew prophets.

USE RHETORICAL QUESTIONS TO TRANSITION

Our discussion of rhetorical questions in the previous chapter has already made the point that rhetorical questions draw the audience into the sermon and make them more persuasively vulnerable to the point being made. Instead of taking or leaving a declarative statement, the question forces the audience to mentally wrestle with the point for themselves. The fact that questions draw the listeners' interest and engage them mentally means that questions will also assist with oral clarity, because a speaker will be

---

6. Gitay, "Prophetic Criticism," 115.

7. Kugel, *The Idea of Biblical Poetry*, 8–12, shows that biblical parallelism is not merely repetition, but that the second element emphasizes and often heightens or further advances the point made by the first element.

LET ME BE CLEAR

clearer to someone who is more actively listening. Sunukjian's advice to use rhetorical questions in transitions from one major move to the next recognizes the reality that at times our listeners' attention will drift. If they have become distracted or disengaged, then transitioning between points is an important time to help them mentally re-engage. Thus, rhetorical questions not only can regather listeners you may have momentarily lost, transitional questions can also help those who are listening move with you from your previous point into your next point with clarity.[8]

All of the prophets use rhetorical questions, often as an emphatic statement, declaring what is self-evident, although not always to clarify a transition. Lundbom cites numerous examples of Jeremiah's use of rhetorical questions, including 2:11, 14, 31, and 32, which do exemplify Sunukjian's premise. "[Jeremiah's] setup questions, in almost every case contain a word or thought link to the preferred subject, which comes next."[9] Lundbom identifies two categories for how Jeremiah does this which nicely support Sunukjian's principles of clarity:

> In one, a single or double question lifts up some paradigmatic behavior, a common happening or something or something built into the natural order, which the prophet then contrasts to the nation's behavior, judged to be scandalous.
>
> The second type is a threefold question in the form *ha-* . . . *'im* . . . *maddua'?*, commonly translated "Is . . . is . . . so why?" or "If . . . if . . . so why?" This form is a signature for Jeremiah. Here two rhetorical questions are a foil for the third, which states the troubling vexation that Jeremiah wants to address.[10]

In Lundbom's first category, the question is transitional and sets up a clear declaration of the problem the prophet now confronts. Or, in Sunukjian's terms, a transitional question sets up a deductive statement and development of the next main point of the sermon. Examples of this occur in Jeremiah 2:11 and 2:32. In Lundbom's second category, the prophet again uses the first two questions as transitional or introductory to the third question which is itself an emphatic and clear statement of the problem, which will then be developed or illustrated more fully. Examples of this category occur in Jeremiah 2:14 and 2:31. In each of these, the use of a rhetorical question is combined with Sunukjian's fourth principle of oral

---

8. Robinson, "Clearly: How to Preach so Everyone Understands," 335.
9. Lundbom, *The Hebrew Prophets*, 191–94.
10. Ibid., 192–93.

clarity: develop main points within the message deductively. With the help of rhetorical questions, Jeremiah makes clear what his next point is, then develops that point further.

Another well-known prophetic example of using rhetorical questions to transition from one point to the next is the book of Habakkuk. When I have preached Habakkuk's sermon, my outline typically looks something like this: "Lord, why don't you *do* something?" (1:1–11), "Lord, how can *you* do *that*?" (1:12—2:20), and "Lord, I will trust you." (3:1–19). Habakkuk's opening questions are well known, for the prophet dares to challenge God himself. Rhetorically, the prophet is likely expressing the questions which are also in the heart of his audience, his complaint is not only his own, it is also "on behalf of his people."[11]

This rhetorical technique, seemingly challenging God by verbalizing what the audience is saying, is effective in drawing the audience in and introducing God's answer to each question. Since the prophet is God's spokesman, the people are ready to hear God's answer to their question from the prophet. Pastorally, we would not assume God's voice in reply, in the same way that Habakkuk does. However, after verbalizing the question as our own, we can then point to the passage and overview how God answers this question. Then, in reading the text, the people hear God's word respond to their question, just as this audience heard God through Habakkuk. This may be one of the closest examples of a prophet exemplifying another of Sunukjian's principles for oral clarity: Give a mini-synopsis of the point of any verses before you read them.[12] Habakkuk posed a question shared by the people as a transition to an answer to that question in a word from God. Similarly, preachers can pose a question which the text will answer, preview how the text will answer that question and then read and exposit the text.

Because the prophets use rhetorical questions so frequently, it is not difficult to find additional examples where they use rhetorical questions to transition to the next move of the sermon.[13] For example, Isaiah does so in chapter 5, which we considered in the previous chapter. "What more was there to do for my vineyard, that I have not done in it? When I looked for it to yield grapes, why did it yield wild grapes? And now I will tell you

11. Thompson, "Prayer, Oracle and Theophany," 34.

12. Sunukjian, *Introduction to Biblical Preaching*, 294.

13. Regt, "Discourse Implications of Rhetorical Questions in Job, Deuteronomy and the Minor Prophets," 71–74, shows how rhetorical questions are used structurally in transitioning from one main section to another in Micah, Nahum, Habakkuk, Zechariah, Haggai and Malachi.

what I will do to my vineyard" (Isa 5:4–5). After announcing the transition by raising the question, "What more could I do?" he begins the next move announcing what he will do.

Malachi puts a slightly different twist on the technique of using rhetorical questions to introduce each new move in the sermon. The prophet brings a series of complaints or disputations against his people. They have overlooked his love (1:2); they dishonor him (1:6); they consider God distant (2:13); they weary him with their words (2:17); they have turned away (3:7), and they have spoken against him (3:13). In each case, immediately following his complaint, he rhetorically restates it as a question coming from the people. Perhaps we could call this a "rhetorical restatement question." For oral clarity, it's a two-in-one. The point is made very clear, and the structure of the message is clear as the prophet progresses from point to point. In addition, the technique is also memorable: you may have called to mind Malachi's unique use of rhetorical questions as soon as I raised the point at the beginning of the paragraph.

PRESENT EACH NEW MAIN POINT IN A DEDUCTIVE MANNER

A sermon or message can be presented either inductively or deductively.[14] In an inductive sermon, the main question to be answered is raised in the introduction and the answer is developed through the main points of the message. This helps maintain tension in the message and helps the audience maintain interest. A deductive sermon reveals the topic and the answer, what you are talking about and what you have to say about it, in the introduction. The main points then further explain and apply that answer to the topic at hand. This works especially well when the audience will question or even disagree with the proposed answer, thus providing tension that gives them a reason to continue listening.

However, regardless of whether the overall sermon is developed inductively or deductively, Sunukjian insists that for oral clarity, each main point should be presented deductively: the overall premise of that main movement should be stated in full sentences before developing the sub points.[15] Chapell agrees, suggesting that each main point should be stated

---

14. Sunukjian, *Biblical Preaching*, 155–60.

15. Ibid., 288. The exception to this principle is if the sub units are a list, in which case they should be presented inductively.

clearly, then developed, illustrated and applied.[16] Deductive development of each main point helps the listeners track through the sub points and understand how they relate to the main point.

Jeremiah appears to use a similar approach, developing individual points deductively, in Jeremiah 2. His first point (2:5–13) is that "they [Judah] went far from me, and went after worthlessness and became worthless" (2:5). This is then validated in that Israel has forgotten the one who faithfully led them out of Egypt and into the land (2:6–7), that they no longer seek him (2:8–9). Such a departure from one's own God to non-gods is remarkable (2:10–11), it is comparable to forsaking living or life-giving water for empty, broken and useless cisterns which can't hold water (2:12–13).

Jeremiah's second main assertion is that instead of receiving the Lord's covenant protection, Israel has become a prey to others: "Why then has he [Israel] become a prey?" (2:14). This point is validated by the roaring of lions, representing harassment from Assyria (2:15),[17] as well as Judah's recent subjugation to Egypt after Josiah's death (2:16–17). Ironically, Judah has sought help from Egypt and Assyria, instead of turning to the Lord (2:19), who has in the past delivered his people from these enemies (2:20–22). This idolatrous trust in others instead of the Lord (2:23–25) will leave them without the Lord's help (2:26–28).

In the third main move of the sermon, the Lord confronts the people's futile protestation that they have not transgressed against the Lord (2:29). The depth of their transgression of the covenant is then developed in detail. They have rebelled against the Lord's previous correction by killing his prophets (2:30). Their departure from the Lord is indefensible (2:31–32), their actions would teach even wicked women a thing or two about treachery, while they brazenly declare their innocence (2:33–35). However, their false trust is Egypt is uncovered and will disappoint them (2:36–37). They have been unfaithful (3:1) which is why they have experienced covenantal chastening (3:2–3), and yet they brazenly suggest God should rescue them even though they will not confess their guilt (3:4–5).

In this sermon, Jeremiah's overall point, the implication that Israel has departed from the faithfulness of her youth is developed inductively, through the three moves I have described above. His initial assertion that

---

16. Chapell, *Christ Centered* Preaching, 168–69. See also Richard, *Scripture Sculpture*, 113.

17. Chisholm, *Handbook on the Prophets*, 156, suggests the lion metaphor could be an allusion to Assyrian invasions of the prior century.

Israel departed from God and went after worthlessness at first appears to refer to Baal worship. However the next point shows this apostasy includes Israel's false confidence in the strength of her surrounding enemies, and is finally shown to also include their presumptuous attitude toward their relationship with the Lord.[18] While these points are revealed inductively through the message, each main point is developed deductively, being clearly stated and then developed and validated in its sub points.

Another good example of each main point being developed inductively is found in the book of Malachi. As mentioned above, Malachi uses rhetorical questions to restate his main points. Then, in the paragraphs that follow this rhetorical question, he answers the question, by developing and demonstrating the validity of his complaint in detail. The overall structure of Malachi is inductive: the main point of Malachi is not revealed until the end of the book. It is a call to return to the fear of the Lord (3:16—4:6) and to remember his covenant which includes all of the preceding points, which have each been developed deductively.

USE KEY LANGUAGE AND PHRASING THROUGHOUT

Another of Sunukjian's principles of oral clarity is to consistently use similar language through the sermon. This principle applies to using similar phrasing from the introduction, through each main point, to the conclusion. Consistent use of similar language can also be applied to each main point's key language being used consistently through the sub-points and illustrations which develop that main point. Similarly, Bryan Chapell urges us to "rain the key words of the subpoints (or the key terms of the main point if there are no subpoints) into the sentences we use to tell the illustration."[19] This aptly describes the prophets. While they don't always develop points in the linear logical way in which we might, the prophets did use consistent

---

18. Noticing how Jeremiah develops his message also protects the expositor from assuming Jeremiah is equally condemning three discrete faults. Because the third point is the inductive climax, more emphasis should be placed here when preaching from this text. God's people have sought other fulfillment and sources of security because they have neglected and presumed upon their unique covenant relationship with God. Rightly sensing the climax of Jeremiah's sermon in the third point, will help me to get the message from this text right in my own sermon from it.

19. Chapell, *Christ-Centered Preaching*, 197

Part Two

language to highlight a theme to provide unity and clarity.[20] Let's turn again to Jeremiah's first sermon to see this in practice.

In Jeremiah 2:5-6, the first main point is stated (using restatement as described above.) The key terms are "went far from me," "went after worthlessness," and "did not say 'where is the Lord?'" which is to say they did not seek the Lord. These key terms (or concepts) are echoed, in reverse order: "The priests did not say where is the Lord" (2:8a), "they went after things that did not profit" (2:8b), and have "forsaken me" (2:14). As he develops this point, the prophet is clearly still talking about the same thing; his audience would not have had trouble following him.

In the introduction (Jer 2:2-3), Jeremiah had subtly introduced his point by describing in romantic and idealistic terms what had once been true.[21] Israel was devoted as a bride; she had followed the Lord in the wilderness, was the first fruits of his harvest, and disaster came on neighboring nations who troubled her. Then, in his sermon he sharply contrasts what had been with the situation as it now is. To do so, he uses key words which evoke the same imagery, even if they are not an exact repetition of the same word or phrasing.[22] He declares, in sharp contrast but in similar terms, that the "devoted bride" has become a whore (2:20), who has loved many foreigners (2:25) and become the bride who has forgotten her attire (2:32) and is now like a divorced wife (3:1). Instead of following the Lord in the wilderness, she has not sought the Lord who "led us in the wilderness" (2:6). She has forsaken the Lord who "led you in the way" (2:17); she has gone her own way in the wilderness (2:24) and the Lord has become as a wilderness to Israel (2:31). In contrast to being a fruitful harvest, they have defiled the plentiful land (2:7) and have become a wild vine (2:21) so that "the showers [needed for a fruitful harvest] have been withheld, and the spring rain has not come" (3:3). Finally, disaster has come upon her at the hands of her oppressive neighbors (2:15-16) and the Lord will not protect them from this trouble (2:27-28).

---

20. However, Susan Niditch cautions that "repetition is not a simple-minded stylistic device that allows an audience to follow a story that is heard rather than read." Niditch, *Oral World and Written Word*, 13-14.

21. Chisholm, *Handbook on the Prophets*, 156, makes clear that Jeremiah did not have a naïve and nostalgic view of Israel's history. Rather he is using this romantically idealistic description of history rhetorically to sharpen the contrast between a once devoted people to a presently apostate people (2:19).

22. Niditch, *Oral World and Written Word*, 13. According to Niditch, "A third variety of repetition involves play on a particular *Leitwort*, or key word."

Jeremiah's contrast of Israel planted as a choice vine only to become a wild vine, builds on the powerful imagery used by Isaiah (Isa 5:1–7), demonstrating another aspect of the repetition of key image—repetition over time. While discussing Ezekiel's borrowing and building upon the vine imagery, Ellen Davis points out that "much of the power of biblical imagery . . . derives from its relation to earlier language." Davis continues:

> He [Ezekiel] shows his genius and his mastery of the tradition by appropriating its symbols, then complicating and deepening them. Even more significantly, he shows his commonality with those to whom the symbols are meaningful and leads them in turn into a more reflective engagement with the tradition.
>
> A second way in which Ezekiel uses familiarity to his advantage is the repetition and variation of his own images. Thus a figure such as a vine is enriched, not only through reverberations with other texts, but also by the echoes set up within Ezekiel's own prophecy.[23]

Pastorally, repeatedly applying the same key images over time has been effective in my preaching ministry. Being convinced that one of the Apostle Paul's central metaphors for the church is family, "the household of God" (1 Tim 3:15), I frequently recall and refer to this imagery in my messages. I borrow this family image used by Paul, building upon it and deepening the church's grasp of it and its impact upon us by varied yet consistent use over time. As a result, the concept of a local church as a local expression of God's extended family has become a central and defining aspect of our church's practical (and practiced) theology.

The prophets' consistent use of metaphors and images, which are close to the people's experience and thus easily understandable, gives further clarity to their sermons. Lundbom agrees that by "lowering the level of abstraction, metaphors make ideas more concrete."[24] Furthermore, metaphors "bring experiences to mind that touch the heart more deeply."[25] Therefore, Sunukjian advises us to "be as picturesque as possible in your explanations. Avoid dictionary definitions and abstract descriptions that cause the eye to glass over. Instead, put a picture in your listeners mind,"[26] because "visual preaching aids clarity."[27]

---

23. Davis, *Swallowing the Scroll*, 93–94.
24. Lundbom, *The Hebrew Prophets*, 181.
25. Chapell, *Christ-Centered Preaching*, 188.
26. Sunukjian, *Biblical Preaching*, 90.
27. Robinson, "Clearly," 334.

Part Two

BUILDING IN STRUCTURAL CLARITY

The use of keywords or consistent language or imagery throughout a main point does more than provide immediate clarity to that concept. The use of keywords or key phrases also shows the prophets intentionally providing a recognizable structure to their sermon which can be perceived and comprehended aurally by their listeners. H. V. D. Parunak explains that the use of key language produces a recognizable pattern which gives unity to a section, showing that it fits together. Furthermore, when the keyword disappears and is replaced by a new key term or phrase, the audience perceives a new pattern, indicating a new structural unit.[28] Parunak's point is that using key terms or words in a recognizable pattern is one way in which the prophets provided clarifying structure in their sermons. The use of repetitive keywords or phrasing to provide a clear structure has already been seen in our discussion of Amos 1–2 in chapter four, where the prophet frames his introduction with the phrase "For three sins . . . even for four."

The prophets also enhanced oral clarity by structuring their overall message or individual points in recognizable patterns. The two of these most commonly observed in biblical literature and in the prophet's sermons are chiasm and alternation.[29] Alternation is a recognizable repetitive pattern, where key words or phrases are repeated in order to provide structure (ABC/A'B'C'). In contrast, Chiasm is a pattern where parallels at the beginning and end of a unit, are repeated toward a center. Chiasm could be a very simple pattern (ABA') or a more complex pattern (ABC/C'B'A' or ABCXC'B'A'). These structural patterns can emphasize a point, mark out peripheral or parenthetical material, indicate divisions, or preview upcoming more detailed exposition.[30]

For example, in Ezekiel 26, the chapter appears to be separated into four recognizable units (26:3–6, 7–14, 15–18, 19–21) by the repetition of the phrase, "thus says the Lord." However, 26:15–18 and 26:19–20 are also structured as individually distinct units by use of a simple inclusio

---

28. Parunak, "Some Axioms for Literary Architecture," 6. See also Parunak, "Transitional Techniques in the Bible," 525–58, for further discussion on the prophets use of keywords to transition from one unit to the next.

29. For a detailed treatment of inclusio and chiasmus in the book of Jeremiah, see Lundbom, *Jeremiah*.

30. Parunak, "Oral Typesetting," 155.

(26:15–18) and then a multi-paneled chiasm (26:19–20).³¹ Visually, the structure looks like this:

15 "Thus says the Lord GOD to Tyre:
  (A) Will not *the coastlands shake at the sound of your fall*, when the wounded groan, when slaughter is made in your midst?
    (B) 16 Then all the princes of the sea will step down from their thrones and remove their robes and strip off their embroidered garments. They will clothe themselves with trembling; they will sit on the ground and tremble every moment and be appalled at you. 17 And they will raise a lamentation over you and say to you,
    "'How you have perished, you who were inhabited from the seas,
    O city renowned, who was mighty on the sea;
    she and her inhabitants imposed their terror on all her inhabitants!
  (A') 18 Now *the coastlands tremble on the day of your fall*, and the coastlands that are on the sea are dismayed at your passing.'
  (A) 19 "For thus says the Lord GOD: *When I make you a city laid waste*,
    (B) like the *cities that are not inhabited*, when I bring up the deep over you, and the great waters cover you,
      (C) 20 then I will make you go down *with those who go down to the pit*,
        (D) *to the people of old*,
          (X) *and I will make you to dwell in the world below*,
        (D') *among ruins from of old*,
      (C') *with those who go down to the pit*,
    (B') so that *you will not be inhabited*;
  (A') but *I will set beauty in the land of the living*.
21 I will bring you to a dreadful end, and you shall be no more. Though you be sought for, you will never be found again, declares the Lord GOD."

The chiastic structure of 26:19–20 separates these verses structurally from the last verse of the chapter, even though 26:21 was not identified as a discrete unit by the structural marker, "thus says the Lord." Parunak concludes that 26:21 actually serves as a conclusion for the entire chapter

---

31. Ibid., 158–59. The inclusio is a simple chiastic form (ABA') and can be used either to emphasize the B panel or can identify the B panel is supplemental or parenthetical material.

and oracle. Ezekiel apparently used both a key phrase and chiasm to clarify the moves of his message.

The prophets also used oral structural markers to emphasize certain parts of a text and to link components together into a larger whole. In our discussion of Isaiah 5 in the previous chapter, it was noted that the prophet had adapted the normal form of the woe oracle in order to emphasize the accusations and heighten the emotional impact of these repetitive accusations upon his audience. In his unexpected clustering of accusations in Isaiah 5:8–23, the prophet has also arranged the accusations to form a parallel chiastic pattern as Chisholm demonstrates:[32]

A Accusation: social injustice [in accumulating property] (v. 8)
* Announcement of judgment (vv. 9–10)
   B Accusation: carousing [drunkenness] (vv. 11–12a)
      C Accusation: failure to recognize the Lord's work (v. 12b)
* Announcement of judgment (vv. 13–17)
      C' Accusation: failure to recognize the Lord's work (vv. 18–21)
   B' Accusation: carousing [mighty men at drinking wine] (v. 22)
A' Accusation: social injustice [in legal corruption] (v. 23)
* Announcement of judgment (vv. 24–30)

In the chiasm, A parallels A', B parallels B', and C parallels C'. Recognizing this chiastic structure helps us to also see parallels in the accusations which would have likely been easily apparent to Isaiah's audience, or at least became apparent to them as they reflected further on what the prophet had said. The unjust accumulation of property (v. 8) was accomplished through the injustice of legal corruption (v. 23). The carousing and drunkenness (vv. 11–12a) have deprived them of the true mighty men they will soon need (v. 22) when judgment comes. Instead of repenting and being prepared, they disregard and ridicule the reality that just God has intervened (12b), and God will intervene in judgment (18–21). Thus chiastic structure makes the central point clear: God will intervene in judgment, while also making clear why that judgment is coming.

Parunak insists that these repetitive patterns (keyword, alternation and chiasm) for oral structure and clarity are not confined to Old Testament Hebrew writings or culture but are a consequence of restricting the resources of language to one (oral or aural) dimension. Thus, they are also

---

32. Chisholm, "Structure, Style, and the Prophetic Message," 51.

evident in the New Testament and are still in use today in written works which are meant to be read aloud and understood aurally, such as editorials, poems and children's books.[33] Therefore, it is not surprising that they should also be used in sermons. For example, Parunak points out that an external inclusio (ABA') being used to mark out parenthetical material is commonly heard today. "After speakers interrupt their train of thought, whether to answer a query or to extemporize, they frequently resume their argument by repeating, often unconsciously, a phrase from just before the interruption."[34]

Perhaps you are thinking that these subtle nuances of chiastic structure in the prophet's sermons are not good examples for us today. After all, they are often not alliterated, or paralleled in ways that obviously stand out and can be easily remembered by the audience. Perhaps that is the point: the prophets don't draw attention to their structure, but instead use structural techniques to more clearly make their point. Perhaps the point is that we don't want the audience to remember the structure and main points of the message so much as to remember, or be influenced by the overall point of the message. As Chapell says, "Although an outline is a logical path to the mind, it is not necessary for a listener to retain its every detail in order for the message to be effective."[35] Robinson provides a good metaphor of the true purpose of the structure of the message:

> Outlines serve as skeletons of thought, and in most sermons, as in most bodies, the skeleton will not be completely hidden. We ought not put the outline on vulgar display, however, as if the skeleton were "Exhibit C, Victim of Starvation." The most effective means of hiding the bare bones of a sermon is not by disposing of the skeleton but by covering it with flesh.[36]

Robinson goes on to say that not many people have "ever been moved to faith by reading an outline of Romans."[37] It is the message, not the structure that is the point, but the structure of the message can either help or

---

33. Parunak, "Some Axioms for Literary Architecture," 10.

34. Parunak, "Oral Typesetting," 162.

35. Chapell, *Christ-Centered Preaching*, 157. Several authors have spoken to the confusion that arises when a catchy alliterated outline is too cute by half and overtakes the main point of the text. See Sunukjian, *Biblical Preaching*, 311–14; Mathewson, "Outlines That Work for You," 360–61.

36. Robinson, *Biblical Preaching*, 139.

37. Ibid.

hinder the clarity of the message. The structure should support the message without overwhelming it. Steven Mathewson advises:

> "Don't try to create outlines people will remember. It took me years of preaching to figure this out. I sincerely believed that listeners would be better for taking my outline points home with them—either in their heads or, better yet, on paper.
>
> ... Alliterating the three main points ... provides a memory aid. But, obviously, this kind of communication is unnatural. It's boring and it doesn't work the way conversation normally flows."[38]

The prophets provide clear structure for their messages, but the structure enhances and clarifies the message, rather than getting in the way. This is what we must learn from the prophets' example in terms of the structure of our sermons. The structure may or may not be memorable, but it must hold up and help communicate the overall point of the message. To this end, we should never look for the three points of any given text we are to preach, but rather ask, how many points, or what sermon structure best develops and communicates the message of this text? We might even find that a sermon structure similar to a Hebrew chiasm, which builds towards and then supportively withdraws from a single central point might be the most effective way to preach the main idea of a passage. After all, if Parunak is right, that chiasm is related to the limitations of oral language rather than being peculiar to Hebrew oral culture, we might be neglecting an important structural tool which the prophets effectively employed.

In this chapter we have surveyed several of the prophets' sermons, identifying rhetorical and structural techniques used by the prophets to make their messages unmistakably clear. It is evident that many of the things which we are urged to do to enhance the clarity of our sermons are the same things which the prophets did. They are a good example for us to refer to and be encouraged by. We can, in some ways and at some level, preach like the prophets. We should not try to imitate them, but we should observe and learn from them.

The more we study and reflect on the rhetorical techniques of the prophets, the more obvious it becomes that these preachers did not simply speak ecstatically however the Spirit moved them. Their sermons show deliberate intentionality. They gave careful thought to how to convey the burden of the Lord. They planned for clarity and persuasive effect. They may

---

38. Mathewson, "Outlines That Work for You," 361.

have even written out their oracles before delivering them.[39] They structured their sermons in a way that would be recognizable and clear to their audience without the use of sermon outlines in the bulletin or a PowerPoint on the screen behind them. They restated key points so that they would not be missed, and they used rhetorical questions and engaging key terms to keep their listeners focused on God's word through them.

Long before Aristotle, the prophets' example demonstrates that "it is not enough to know what we ought to say; we must also say it as we ought . . . the way in which a thing is said does affect its intelligibility."[40] Their example encourages us to intentionally plan the structure, the moves, the transitions and the delivery of our sermons so that God's word through us will be heard as clearly as possible.

---

39. Numerous scholars have departed from the long held view that the prophets' oracles were only written down long after the prophets spoke. Lessing, *Orality in the Prophets*, 152–65, provides a good overview of the progression of scholarship in this area. Niditch, in *Oral World and Written Word*, 117, believes that prophetic speeches were likely written down and then performed orally. Ben Zvi, in "Introduction: Writings, Speeches, and the Prophetic Books," 16–17, suggests "It is reasonable to assume that an authoritative written text becomes the starting point for the oral performances of the literati and for the aurallity of an audience." A clear example of the prophets words being written down to be orally delivered occurs in Jeremiah 36:2, where Baruch is instructed by Jeremiah to write on a scroll all the words he has spoken, in order for the message to be read aloud to the king. Lessing, in *Orality in the Prophets*, 164, concludes, "Therefore, it might be suggested that prophets composed their sermons in writing in order to deliver them orally, either through reading or memorization."

40. Aristotle, *Rhetoric*, 120–21.

8

Up Close and Personal

Prophetic preaching is about the "today-ness" of divine reality when Christian preachers respond to Scripture as Old Testament prophets did when they heard the word of the Lord. When prophets declared, "Listen to the word of the Lord," they had a conviction that God had spoken and was now present, expressing himself through the prophet's words.

MICHAEL J. QUICKE[1]

Life changing preaching does not talk to people about the Bible. Instead, it talks to people about themselves—their questions, hurts, fears, and struggles—from the Bible.

HADDON ROBINSON[2]

We are a prophetic minority who must speak into a world that is . . . exactly what Jesus promised us the world must be.

RUSSELL MOORE[3]

The prophets spoke for God in a specific time to a specific people. Because we are not in that same day or share the same experiential

---

1. Quicke, *360-Degree Preaching*, 20.
2. Robinson, "Blending Bible Content and Life Application," 299.
3. Bailey, "Moore on the Margins," 30.

background as the prophets' audience, the prophets' messages are more difficult for us to understand. However, this is partly because they spoke so relevantly to their contemporary situation. Whatever else can be said about the prophets' sermons, they were unavoidably relevant to their intended audience; they spoke specifically to their audience's current situations.

In preaching, relevance refers to how the message relates to the matters at hand for the listeners. "Relevance explains to our listeners how what happened in Bible times can happen today."[4] A sermon is relevant when the truth of God's word intersects with the realities of the listener's experience. Relevance has occurred when the preacher declares "You are the man!" and David is compelled to reply, "I have sinned against the Lord" (2 Sam 12:1–15).

As God's messengers, the prophets spoke the timeless truth of God to the present situation. "The prophet's eye is directed to the contemporary scene; the society and its conduct are the main theme of his speeches."[5] Sensing says that the prophets forged together three elements: the covenant tradition from Moses, the concrete realities of some particular situation and God's new word for the present day.[6] If we adjust the arrangement of Sensing's three elements slightly, we could say that God's new word for the present day was the preaching of God's revelation given through Moses to the concrete realities of some particular contemporary situation. That is to say that the prophets preached from special revelation given up to a thousand years earlier to a present situation in a way that spoke relevantly to the specific circumstances of their contemporaries.

Understanding that the prophets preached Moses to their contemporary generation means that they were not so much futuristic seers as they were applicational preachers. Barton concludes that the prophets were not philosophical soothsayers but applicationally relevant messengers of God in their own day:

> One of the great insights of modern critical study has been that the great classical prophets were not clairvoyants providing their devotees with arcane information about the future or about the mysteries of the universe, but spokesmen for a moral and demanding God who addressed themselves to the state of Israelite society

---

4. Veerman, "Apply Within," 285.
5. Heschel, *The Prophets*, 21.
6. Sensing, "A Call to Prophetic Preaching," 143–44.

Part Two

in their own day and uttered rebukes and warnings of immediate application.[7]

Similarly, Clendenen argues that the prophetic books are essentially "coherent behavioral exhortation" and that even the future predictions contained in them should be understood as supplemental material that is immediately relevant to the exhortation being given to the audience:

> Recognizing the nature of the prophetic books as coherent behavioral exhortation, that is, hortatory discourse, has important implications. In such discourses the most prominent element is naturally the behavioral change or changes being advocated. All other elements in the discourse must relate to one or more of the commands or exhortations, and it would be a misuse of scripture to listen to only one of the supplemental elements, such as predictive prophecy, without relating it to the central message of the book.[8]

Therefore, instead of focusing on the future fulfillment of prophetic predictions as the main message, we should look more carefully into how that the future prediction was relevant to the audience's current behavior. Apparently the prophets understood that what a person believes about the future will make a difference in what they choose to do in the present.

Just as the prophets spoke relevantly to specific behavioral issues, they also spoke relevantly to their immediate audience and context. Lundbom declares that the prophets' messages were dynamic, delivered to a specific audience at a particular moment of time, rather than a static message of general truth which is divorced from any specific historical situation.[9] The prophets did not give a general message about Moses's instructions to another people hundreds of years earlier; they spoke from Moses to the people in their day. Lundbom references Gerhard von Rad's observation of the prophets' situational relevance:

> Here, it is all-important not to read this message as if it consisted of timeless ideas, but to understand it as the particular word relevant to a particular hour in history, which therefore cannot be replaced by any other word. The prophetic word—far more than any of the other forms of speech used by Jahwism—has its origin

---

7. Barton, *Oracles of God*, 131–32. Similarly, Brueggemann, *Prophetic Imagination*, 2, says, "While the prophets are future-tellers, they are concerned with the future as it impinges on the present."

8. Clendenen, "Textlinguistics and Prophecy," 390.

9. Lundbom, *The Hebrew Prophets*, 142.

in an impassioned dialogue; yet the dialogue never tries to climb into the realm of general religious truth, but instead uses even the most suspect means to tie the listening partner down to his particular time and place in order to make him understand his own situation before God.[10]

Donald Sunukjian's description of a biblical preacher is one who says, "Look what God is saying . . . to us."[11] He urges us to be careful to be true to the inspired text, to preach the exact meaning which God intended.[12] However, in the present tense of his description, "what God is saying," as well as in his contemporary thrust, "to us," he stresses the present day relevance of the biblical sermon. God's inerrant word is as relevant to the human condition today as when it was first given in the process of progressive revelation. As Robinson says, "We don't 'make the Bible relevant'; we show its relevance."[13] However, the prophets take pains to speak relevantly because often "relevance must be demonstrated rather than assumed evident to the audience."[14]

Sunukjian demonstrates that Jesus and the apostles believed that the Hebrew Scriptures, which were written centuries earlier, were directly relevant to the pressing issues of their day:

> When the Pharisees challenged Jesus as to why he was allowing his disciples to pick grain on the Sabbath (Matt 12:1–2), he replied, "Haven't you read what David did when . . . ?" (v. 3). In Jesus's mind, God was giving them the answer to their question through an incident recorded a thousand years earlier.
>
> Similarly, Paul, referring to the historical events of Exodus and Numbers, says, "These things . . . were written down as warnings for us" (1 Cor 10:1l). Through accounts written 1,500 years earlier, God was speaking to Gentiles in Paul's day—and to us, now.[15]

---

10. von Rad, *The Theology of Israel's Prophetic Traditions*, 129, quoted in Lundbom, *The Hebrew Prophets*, 142.

11. Sunukjian, *Biblical Preaching*, 9.

12. An important step towards ensuring a message is both true to the text and relevantly stated, explained and applied today is to match the original purpose of the text with its original audience to a similar purpose of God for the contemporary audience. See Chapell, *Christ-Centered Preaching*, 48–52; Greidanus, *Preaching Christ from the Old Testament*, 287; Richard, *Scripture Sculpture*, 79–83, and especially Kuruvilla, *Privilege the Text*.

13. Robinson, "Convictions of Biblical Preaching," 23.

14. Willhite, "Connecting with Your Congregation," 96.

15. Sunukjian, *Biblical Preaching*, 11.

PART TWO

The apostle Peter also asserts that the prophets, in their earlier ministry, were not only serving their own generation, they were serving generations which would come long after them. The prophets' ministry was intended by God to be especially relevant for those who would live and believe God's word many hundreds of years later:

> Concerning this salvation, the prophets who prophesied about the grace that was to be yours searched and inquired carefully, inquiring what person or time the Spirit of Christ in them was indicating when he predicted the sufferings of Christ and the subsequent glories. It was revealed to them that they were serving not themselves but you, in the things that have now been announced to you through those who preached the good news to you by the Holy Spirit sent from heaven, things into which angels long to look (1 Pet 1:10–12).

According to Peter, the message which turned the world upside down (Acts 17:6) in the first century was the preaching of the gospel based upon the word of God given through the prophets. This word from God, originally given through the prophets many centuries earlier, was obviously relevant to people living in the first century. Therefore, we do not need to question whether the word of God is relevant so many years after it was given. The issue is whether our preaching of the word of God is relevant to our listeners today.

A common oversimplification is to understand relevance as merely referring to specific application. Sometimes we might interchange the terms relevancy and application. However, as Sunukjian says:

> Relevancy is broader than application. Application implies something for the listener to do. Relevancy simply shows how the message connects to life. Apart from any behavior we may eventually urge upon the listener, the whole message should repeatedly picture how the biblical situations or materials are duplicated in contemporary experience.[16]

In fact, application can be specific but not relevant if it does not intersect with a listener's own life situation. For instance, if the application I suggest in a sermon relates to specific actions husbands and wives can take, but I am speaking to high school students, my application might be specific and contemporary, yet not relevant. In order to show the relevance of God's truth, the preacher must show how this truth relates to the listeners' own lives, rather than merely to somebody's life somewhere.

16. Ibid., 106.

Furthermore, if relevance is only considered in the application of the sermon, that application will lack compelling biblical authority because the explanation and illustrations of the biblical principle did not intersect with the listener's experience. As a result, listeners who have not been persuaded that the message related to them as it unfolds, may not be compelled to act on the specific and even relevant application that is exhorted. This is because the application may seem to be dropped out of the sky at the end of the sermon, if it was not founded upon relevant explanations and illustrations of God's truth throughout the sermon. We best provide people the opportunity to live by faith when they clearly see the relevant explanation of God's word leading to relevant application in which they can participate. As Sunukjian says, "Our sermon must be an extended meditation on God's truth, which will result in an understanding not only of *what* is said, but also *why* it is good wisdom, and *where* it is operating or can operate in our lives."[17]

A relevant sermon states its points in fresh and contemporary terms, develops those points with explanations and illustrations which intersect with the listeners' experiences, and provide clear and specific ways in which the listeners can respond to God's message, in their context. Relevancy means that "all through the message—from the opening and all through the concepts—we constantly ask, 'What does this look like in real life? How does it show up in everyday situations?'"[18] In this we share some continuity with the prophets because this is what the prophets did and it is also what we must do.

MAIN POINTS THAT SPEAK TO MAIN STREET

The truth we seek to convey must be conveyed in contemporary language. The main points of the sermon need to be stated in main street terms. Winfred Neely says:

> In addition to being memorable and concise, each main point should be stated in language that is fresh, up-to-date, and contemporary. The living God is not merely the God of yesterday; He is the God of today. Christ is our contemporary, and this great reality must come across in the way we state our main points. For starters, state the main points in the present tense. Great preaching

---

17. Sunukjian, "Questions That Put Muscle on Bone," 349.
18. Ibid., 348.

is always in the present tense, always speaks to the concerns of the day, and speaks in the thought-forms and language of the day. It is never antiquarian, never nerdy nostalgic after the past, never neutral or detached in its attitude.[19]

The prophet Haggai, in his series of brief messages, demonstrates several different ways to communicate a main point in a relevant manner which speaks directly to what is going on in the hearts of his audience. In his first message Haggai uses a statement which the people have been presently saying, "the time has not yet come to rebuild the house of the Lord" (1:2), to frame his point that now is the time to "build the house" (1:8). It is as if he has been reading their email, or listening in on their coffee shop conversations. Malachi applies the same technique. He refers to things which the people are saying at least fourteen times in fifty-five verses. Obadiah uses the same method to confront Edom's proud self-assurance, addressing those "who say in your heart, 'Who will bring me down to the ground?'" by asserting that "I will bring you down, declares the Lord" (1:3–4). The prophets made their point in relevant terms by speaking to the people about what the people have been speaking about.

In his second message (1:12–15), Haggai seems to know what they are thinking and what they need to hear. Just as in the first case, the preacher speaks with compelling relevance because he speaks to what is currently going on inside his audience's head. However, in this case, the prophet is not using their words against them, but using his understanding of what they are thinking to say what they most need to hear. Assurance from the Lord that "I am with you" (1:13) speaks directly to their doubts and echoes the Lord's promise to Moses when he was called (Exod 3:12). By knowing and thus speaking what they need to hear, the prophet gives them hope while also connecting them back to the foundations of God's covenant with them.

When God's Spirit speaks to his people, through his messenger, what they need to hear, it is transforming. "The Lord stirred up the spirit" of the leaders and the remnant (Hag 1:14), giving a divine boost to human obedience.[20] This is the essence of prophetic preaching: the messenger of the

---

19. Neely, "Sermons That Move," 325.

20. Chisholm, *Handbook on the Prophets*, 452. Chisholm also notes that the Lord's divine enablement follows the people's initial obedience. The audience also has an impact on whether a message stirs hearts or falls flat, based on how they are responding to God's word, whether they have "ears to hear."

Lord speaks the Lord's message and the Spirit of the Lord uses the speaking of God's word to stir the spirits of those who hear. This is what preaching pastors must do, and what we pray the Lord will do when we do it. "The LORD stirred up ... the spirit of all the remnant of the people" (Hag 1:14), is an earlier example of what Paul described happening when we preach like the prophets, and it is what I want to happen when I preach: "But if all prophesy, and an unbeliever or outsider enters, he is convicted by all, he is called to account by all, the secrets of his heart are disclosed, and so, falling on his face, he will worship God and declare that God is really among you" (1 Cor 14:25).

In his third message, in Haggai 2:1–9, the prophet speaks to the situation as the people see it. He confronts the dissonance between the noble proposition of building the Lord's temple with their current disappointing reality. With "the smaller size of the overall complex, the chipped stones and the lack of gold, the people felt this structure was an embarrassment."[21] In the midst of their discouragement, the prophet strengthens them by reminding them of the covenant he made with them when they came out of Egypt and the accompanying glory of his divine presence. He redirects their focus from the glory of Solomon's structure to the greater glory of the Lord's Shekinah presence. This is not simply rehearsing history; he is showing what happened before in the Bible can also happen here.

This is especially relevant to his audience who are looking at what they are building and thinking, "This will never be anything glorious." The prophet reminds them that a tent in the wilderness had the glory of God's presence and that one day this temple would be visited by a greater glory. Peter does a similar thing when he reminds dispersed and ostracized Jewish Christians that they are a "holy priesthood" and that their costly obedience of faith is a "spiritual sacrifice" (1 Peter 2:5). Haggai is doing what Chapell also recommends: "By mentally identifying the struggles of persons to whom a biblical principle applies, a preacher naturally connects the situations parishioners face and the guidance a text offers."[22]

Similar to the prophets' awareness of what their audience was thinking, Keith Willhite advises preachers that during sermon preparation they should anticipate what their audience is thinking and how listeners might react to their message:

---

21. Smith, *The Prophets as Preachers*, 306.
22. Chapell, *Christ-Centered Preaching*, 217.

Part Two

In sermon preparation one may ask, what is the major claim of this sermon? Once that claim is clear, the question is, how might listeners challenge this claim? (They may say, "Is that true?" "Prove it." "But it doesn't really work that way." "What has happened to those who have tried this?" "Can anyone really do that?") Next, the preacher can reason, what kinds of evidence will the listeners demand in order for them to accept the claim?

By asking such questions, the potential communicative benefits include a more precise sermonic claim, evidence that is germane to the audience's likely challenges, elimination of irrelevant supporting (actually non-supporting) material, and acceptance of the sermon's claim. By achieving these benefits, the relevance of Bible expositors' messages should become more apparent to their listeners.[23]

A final way Haggai enhances relevance to his audience is by coming near to their experience. He asks if holy meat can make other things holy if they touch it and if someone who is unclean can make holy articles also unclean by contact (2:11–13). The question is addressed to the priests because it is their area of expertise, but it is something the people would have seen occur, perhaps having become unclean themselves by coming in contact with something that was unclean. It is also close to the entire audience's experience and interest in that they are working on rebuilding the temple, the societal center of holiness and ritual cleansing. Perhaps they are also thinking among themselves, "How can this temple ever be holy if it is built by our unclean hands?" When Haggai states the main point, he uses the same language he used in the experiential lead-in: "So is it with this people, and with this nation before me, declares the Lord, and so with every work of their hands. And *what they offer there is unclean.*" (2:14, emphasis mine).

In each of these cases the prophet introduced his main point in a way that is relevant to his audience. First, he used current conversations to introduce the point—their own words are preached to them. Next we see that he knew what was going on with his audience and thus knew how to speak to an unspoken need: discouragement. Third, he spoke to the situation as the people saw it; he took "into account the view from the pew."[24] Finally, he connected his point to a shared experience. "Listeners who experience concepts—even vicariously—are more greatly impacted than those who consider words and ideas in the abstract.[25] After making his point by re-

23. Willhite, "Connecting with Your Congregation," 110.
24. Koessler, "View from the Pew," 126.
25. Chapell, *Christ-Centered Preaching*, 185.

lating it to his listeners' experience, Haggai then proceeds to develop that point in a similar manner. In the next section we will see that just as the main points need to be communicated in relevant terms, they also need to be developed or validated in ways that are relevant to the listeners.

SHARPENING THE POINT

Sunukjian says there are three questions that should be considered in developing the main point: "What do I need to explain?," "Do we really believe it?," and "What does doing this look like in real life?"[26] We will consider ways in which the prophets did the first two, explaining and convincing, in this section. Then we will consider how they gave relevant application in the following section.

In Haggai 2:10–19, after the prophet made his point in terms relevant to the experience of his audience (2:11–14), it appears that his immediate concern is that they might not believe him, they might not buy it. His point needs further validation or proof. The proposition that they have been unholy or unclean by their neglect of the temple could be validated by showing how that uncleanness has affected other aspects of life. Haggai provides supporting examples from their own experience: the lack of fruitfulness they have seen in their fields. He gives one specific example after another: poor wheat and barley harvests, fewer and smaller grapes that yield little juice, natural disasters that have ruined production and orchards that are barren (2:15–17,19). Then Haggai connects this lack of prosperity to the fact that they had not been about the Lord's work on his house (2:15–16). Their own experience validates Haggai's point: they do not have covenant fruitfulness because they have neglected covenant faithfulness.

By evoking the real current situation, the preacher does two things: he speaks to people about their present concerns and he shows that he is connected and aware with what is going on in real life. "The extent to which preachers keep specifics in touch with the more common concerns in a congregation, the more their applications will speak to all."[27] Listeners have more confidence that God's word speaks to their world when the preacher demonstrates that he understands both God's word and their world. Sunukjian has applied "Opinion Leadership" research to show that: "Listeners respect a speaker who is aware of what they are aware of. They

---

26. Sunukjian, *Biblical Preaching*, 87–88.
27. Chapell, *Christ-Centered Preaching*, 217.

have confidence in a man who knows the same things they know, whose wide-ranging interests reveal a familiarity with their world of news, jobs, stresses and personal situations."[28]

There is a third thing Haggai does by illustrating his point from his listeners' experience. Since the need in this case is not to explain, but to persuade, he is using these illustrations from their experience to persuade them. He is saying, "Come, on, you've seen the truth of what I'm telling you." Confronting people with the reality of their own experience, without the qualifications and rationalizations they have indulged themselves in can be very persuasive. Chapell suggests this is an important aspect of real-life illustrations:

> Because life experiences inform our souls, our psyches, and our thoughts, citations of such experiences function as basic tools of communication. Illustrations persuade, stimulate involvement, touch the heart, stir the will, and result in decisions. Thus, the primary purpose of illustration is not to clarify but to motivate. Preachers who fail to understand this will assume that when the point they are making is clear, they do not need an illustration. Preachers who grasp the true power and purposes of illustration know that the most clear points often deserve the best illustrations to make the truth as significant to the hearer as it is in Scripture.[29]

Another way that the prophets developed and validated their point was by using vivid concrete illustrations and powerful metaphors. Jeremiah underscored the foolishness of trusting foreign powers who were destined to destruction by describing their coming defeat "with graphic rhetorical imagery" and Nahum's "graphic picture of Assyria's demise functioned as a persuasive reason to accept Nahum's new view on Nineveh."[30] Joel uses the ravages of a locust plague to help those who have shared that experience visualize the terrors of a coming invading army, which they may not have experienced before. Ezekiel's well-known graphic images include the uselessness of a vine branch as wood (Ezek 15), the child who is raised up to be a bride but becomes a whore (Ezek 16) and the valley of dry bones (Ezek 37).

This last example, the dry bones, would be especially relevant as an image of death beyond revival to any who had participated in the reburial

---

28. Sunukjian, "The Credibility of the Preacher," 260.
29. Chapell, *Christ-Centered Preaching*, 186.
30. Smith, *The Prophets as Preachers*, 163, 223.

of dried bones into an ossuary.³¹ In Jewish practice, upon death a body was placed on a shelf in a family tomb. A year later, after the flesh had disintegrated, the dried bones were gathered and placed in an ossuary. This last act of loving grief closed the door on any lingering denial of death and any hope of the person being revived. If Lazarus's revival seemed impossible to Martha after just four days (John 11:39), then the revival of dry bones would be much more impossible (Ezek 37:2–3). The point is that this would be both cognitively and emotionally understood, especially by the older persons who hear Ezekiel describe his vision, because they have shared experience with the image he employs. They have already reburied a loved one's bones. In this context of shared experience, Ezekiel's image becomes a powerful testimony of God's ability to revive Israel no matter how irretrievable their situation seems.

It is easy to demonstrate that the prophets used figurative language. But we might miss the important point that the images used are chosen for their relevance in developing the point for their audience. The prophet's use of metaphor and simile show that they are intentionally relevant to their audience, because figurative language must evoke a shared understanding between speaker and listener in order to communicate effectively. Commenting on Amos's graphic simile of a shepherd unable to rescue a victim from a predator, Gitay explains:

> Figurative language is an integral part of culture, it is a language which communicates between speaker and audience in the most natural way. Thus the known picture embodied in the simile (cf. 1 Sam 17:34; Isa 31:4) is not the performer's creation and, therefore, by its very nature invokes an "image." ... Because images are evoked rather than created by the performer, the participation of the audience is critical: the artist requires the active assistance of the members of the audience in the transformation of plot clichés into vivid images.³²

The implied warning we must take away from Gitay's explanation is to be sure that images and figurative language we might use in preaching are images and experiences that are shared with our audience. Otherwise our words are merely cliché, which tells the listener that what we have is not relevant to them. As Chapell concludes, "We understand most fully what

---

31. For a detailed treatment of burial and reburial practices in Israel, see Evans, *Jesus and the Ossuaries*.

32. Gitay, "Amos's Art of Speech," 308.

is real to us ... it is only when a truth touches us experientially or when we sense the impact it could have on us that we can comprehend it fully."[33] Images that are not based on shared emotional experiences are less likely to move the audience to action.

Even with shared experiences, effective illustration does more than just compare or describe a parallel; it should allow the audience to emotionally feel the point. Chapell explains that there is a difference between describing how deeply moved he was when doctors were setting his son's broken arm, and describing the factors in the events that fueled his emotions, because those details enabled the listeners to feel with him. "To recreate the moving situation is quite different from testifying to having been deeply moved."[34] This is what Jeremiah does in his sermon concerning the drought (Jer 14), as described by Gitay:

> He picks a familiar motif, almost routine in this area of Judah on the border of the desert. But, by dwelling on the subject, by depicting the pain and despair of human being and animal, by portraying concrete images, individual episodes with which the audience is able to identify, by creating an entire world picture, Jeremiah acts on his audiences emotions.[35]

Thus, Jeremiah invokes descriptive emotional images from their audience's world and experiences in order to make abstract points concrete on both the intellectual and emotional levels. Main points which were stated in relevant terms are also clarified and validated in ways that directly relate to their listeners. By relevantly stating and validating their message, the prophets laid a solid foundation for the clear and specific ways in which they also call the people to respond.

"WHAT SHALL WE DO?"

When God has made his point, when his word has been prophetically preached to the matter at hand and the point relevantly developed, the audience will need to know how God expects them to respond. Just as the prophets confronted the specific sin of a particular audience, they are equally specific and relevant when calling for a response. In this section

---

33. Chapell, *Christ-Centered Preaching*, 184.
34. Ibid., 195.
35. Gitay, "Rhetorical Criticism and the Prophetic Discourse," 18.

we will consider the specific and relevant call to response in several of the prophets' sermons because the prophets can be useful examples to us of effective relevant application.

In Isaiah chapter seven, the prophet comes to Judah's young king Ahaz who is anxious about a threatened invasion by Syria and Israel (Isa 7:1,2). Ahaz intends to find security for his reign by buying protection from Assyria (2 Kgs 16:7). Isaiah forcefully declares that Israel and Syria's threat to the Davidic line will not stand (cf. Jer 33:19–20), and then urges specific application directly relevant to the situation at hand. He urges Ahaz to ask God for a validating sign because it is imperative that he believe God's word (Isa 7:9–10). The message from God is relevant, whether Ahaz believes it or not; so when Ahaz rejects a sign for himself, Isaiah turns and gives a sign to the whole house of David (7:13–14). Ironically, the sign which is given ultimately points to the righteous son of David, who would ultimately succeed Ahaz and who will trust himself to the Lord (Isa 53:10).

Isaiah has spoken specifically and relevantly to the political situation of the day and to Ahaz's personal need to believe God's word. Common concerns of the day can be important points of connection to God's truth. "In times of crisis, people listen for a voice. They're tuned to receive messages of hope, courage, God's purposes, and meaning."[36]

Another example of an exhortation to a specific response could be offered from the book of Habakkuk. In the first two chapters, Habakkuk argues with God concerning Judah's approaching doom at the hands of Babylon. The high point of the book comes when we see Habakkuk's response of faith in the third chapter. He alludes to God's redemptive history with Israel (Hab 3:2–15), and then closes with a very specific and relevant description of the kinds of circumstances in which his faith in the Lord will stand firm (3:16–19). This kind of specificity about loss of harvests and livestock will help his audience exercise the same kind of faith in the same kinds of circumstances. Isaiah and Habakkuk remind us that the word of God is relevant to the most pressing matters of the day.

Jeremiah also provided application relevant to a specific situation. At the beginning of the reign of Zedekiah there is apparently a celebration with emissaries from the surrounding nations (Jer 27:1–4). On this occasion Jeremiah fashioned yoke bars as an object lesson, and declared to all the emissaries from the surrounding nations that they should submit to Babylon and not resist (27:4–7). They are warned that "any nation" who

---

36. MacDonald, "Speaking into Crisis," 641.

will not submit to God's decree concerning Babylon will utterly fall, so they must not listen to lies told by false prophets (27:8–11). Then, having spoken in general terms to the nations, Jeremiah applies that general message specifically to Judah, which was likely his true audience all along. He warns King Zedekiah against the false prophets who have not been sent by the Lord (27:12–15), and he warns the priest and all the people about specific false prophecies which are currently being circulated (27:16–22). Then, Jeremiah's message tightens even further, focusing on the false prophet Hananiah (28:1–16) and giving very specific instructions to Israelites in exile, since Judah must submit to Babylon for seventy years (29:1–10).

One of the things which Jeremiah does is in his application is to speak specifically to a variety of people. While his exhortation to the nations may be a rhetorical ploy, he does give specific relevant application to the king, the priests, the people, and to Hananiah. In applying the principle to various groups, the prophet gives us an example of what Sunukjian advocates: apply the truth to several different demographics within the listening audience.[37] Extending the application to multiple persons also helps to clarify the application and extend its reach to those not specifically mentioned. Chapell recommends that preachers provide a clear concrete situation in which the principle applies, and then "unroll the initial concrete example into further situational possibilities by briefly mentioning other situations or struggles common in the congregation to which the biblical truth of the text applies." He explains: "The initial [detailed] situation makes the principle real, the unrolled specifics make it relevant to all."[38]

One of the indications that Jeremiah's application is clear, specific and relevant is that it is so urgently opposed by the false prophet, Hananiah. In fact, this rejection of the message is as specific as the original message; Hananiah even breaks the yoke bars Jeremiah had made for an object lesson (Jer 28:10). Jeremiah's relevant declaration and application have effectively threatened the status quo and cannot be ignored.

Another example of explicit, relevant application that results in specific opposition occurs after Amos's condemnation of Israel's idolatry and the prediction of the Lord's judgment upon Jeroboam II (Amos 7:7–9). The priest of Bethel sends word to King Jeroboam concerning Amos's words (7:10–11), and his tattling betrays the fact that he heard Amos clearly and

---

37. Sunukjian, *Biblical Preaching,* 113–20. See also Overdorf, *Applying the Sermon,* 123–30.

38. Chapell, *Christ-Centered Preaching,* 225.

understood his words to be threateningly relevant. Chapell warns that application is the point at which preachers will often experience passive or active resistance from their audience: "Sound application ventures out of hypothetical abstraction and elbows its way into business practices, family life, social relationships, societal attitudes, personal habits, and spiritual priorities. Application disrupts lives and as a result is the point at which listeners are most likely to tune out a sermon."[39]

He urges us to not shy away from the true relevance of scripture in order to avoid resistance, but he also urges us to take care that any offense taken concerns the truth itself and not our failure to present it wisely and well:

> If a friend were to come to our door one evening and confess that his teenage son is destroying his family, we would invite the friend to sit at our kitchen table, and we would talk plainly. The hurt in our friend's eyes would dissuade us from pompous idealisms, the need to offer real help would make us turn to the Bible for practical aid, and our friendship would keep us speaking with love even if we had to say hard things. The best preaching offers no less. Application presented as though we are speaking to a friend across a kitchen table has more spiritual potential than a dozen sermons designed for delivery from Mount Sinai.[40]

Specific ways which Chapell suggests to best prepare the way for relevant application which may be resisted by the listener include having a conclusive argument which makes the truth undeniably clear, and short-circuiting negative emotions with disarming illustrations.[41] Jeremiah seems to use similar techniques in his confrontation with Hananiah. He disarmingly declares that he wishes Hananiah's optimistic denial could be true (Jer 28:6). He further strengthens his authority by pointing out that Hananiah's track record in predicting peace must be compared against the reliability of the Lord's prophets' previous predictions of judgment which have come to pass (Jer 28:7–9).

Other prophets also give us clear examples of specific and relevant application in their preaching. Malachi speaks clearly against unfaithfulness in Israel and applies his principle specifically to those who have taken foreign wives and to those who have divorced the wives of their youth (Mal 2:11–16). Later, he specifically confronts their unfaithfulness in another

---

39. Ibid., 228.
40. Ibid., 234–35.
41. Ibid., 229–34.

sphere—their failure to bring in tithes from their harvests. His message is relevant all the way through: from the charge, through what they should do in response, to what specifically the resultant blessing would look like if they do obey (Mal 3:7–12).[42]

Since the prophets are rhetorical masters of irony, it is ironic that one of their more common types of specific and relevant application is the implied application. This is the case where the charge is very specifically made concerning all of the things which they should not be doing, and for which judgment is coming. The implied application is "repent and stop doing these things." The implied application is still specific and relevant because the charge or accusation which implies the correct response is specific and relevant. In one example of this in the book of Zephaniah, after a specific detailing of charges and pronouncements of judgment (Zeph 1:2–18) there is a more generic applicational exhortation (2:1–3). The people who will hear God's word are exhorted to "do his just commands, seek righteousness and humility," to possibly escape the coming judgment. In such cases the specific and relevant condemnations of sin become, for those who will hear, a specific and relevant call to repentance. Thus, whether their applications were explicit or implied, the prophets were specifically relevant.

In this chapter we have seen that the prophets preached with relevance to the specific situations faced by their listeners. They didn't keep a safe or respectful distance, but got up close and personal. Their messages were relevant in how they gained attention, how they stated their points, how they developed or validated their message, and the specific and relevant ways in which they called the people to respond. The prophets are helpful examples and encouragements for us to press after the same compelling and specific relevance in our preaching today.

---

42. Sunukjian, *Biblical Preaching*, 101–7, provides several good examples which demonstrate the persuasive benefit of providing specific examples of what relevant application looks like and what specific results might follow.

9

Show and Tell

...prophets are, to be sure, messengers of the spoken word. But the prophets also make statements not consisting of words, or other statements that supplement the words they speak. The prophets and their predecessors, being men and women of the "spirit," were from the earliest times given to dramatic behavior. For them, the prophetic message was more than words.

JACK LUNDBOM[1]

What you have learned and received and heard and seen in me—
practice these things and the God of Peace will be with you.

PHILIPPIANS 4:9

I can't read Psalm 16 without pausing at verse six: "The lines have fallen to me in pleasant places; indeed I have a beautiful inheritance." In the mid-nineties I sat in a church in southern Africa. A beloved former pastor was our visiting preacher and Psalm 16 was his text. Several months earlier he had awoken in the middle of the night to find his wife struggling for her last breaths. Theirs was a sweet marriage and they shared a wonderful life of ministry together, most recently at the denomination's flagship Bible college. Suddenly he was left with three teens, alone. She was too abruptly taken away. None of us could comprehend it. This was the first time we had

---

1. Lundbom, *The Hebrew Prophets*, 208.

seen him since it had happened, and this was his message to us: "The lines have fallen to me in pleasant places; indeed I have a beautiful inheritance."

My friend's message that morning still impacts me, because I both saw and heard that out of his heartbreak he clung tenaciously to hope. He exemplified the truth that "Hope stands as the supreme gift a preacher can offer a congregation while speaking from the shadowy valleys."[2] He had leaned heavily upon, and was living out, the word of hope he had for us: God could be trusted in the deepest and darkest circumstances, and his promised inheritance was better than anything else for which our hearts might be tempted to settle. There was a congruence of his life and his message that was a far more powerful witness to us than either would have been independently. He modeled for me Paul's words to Timothy: "You, however, have followed my teaching, my conduct, my aim in life, my faith, my patience, my love, my steadfastness, my persecutions and sufferings that happened to me at Antioch, at Iconium, at Lystra—which persecutions I endured; yet from them all the Lord rescued me" (2 Tim 3:10–11). Earlier in his ministry, Paul had closed his urgent appeal to the Galatian Christians with a reference to his personal and costly commitment to the true gospel: "From now on let no one cause me trouble, for I bear on my body the marks of Jesus" (Gal 6:17). David Day, in *Preaching with all You've Got*, concludes that no one would doubt that Paul's life matched Paul's words.[3]

These examples from Paul remind us that there is great power in a life which has lived in the truth of the message preached. The example of the prophets demonstrates this as well. The prophets' ministry was not only verbal; the prophets both show and tell. On occasion their own lives become an illustration, an object lesson, and at times an extended parable of the message God gives them to preach. Or, to come at it from the other direction, the prophets at times preach out of the life experience into which God has sovereignly directed them.

It might be helpful to clarify in advance that I am not suggesting that the preacher's experience should ever supplant the word of God as the message. Paul confirms that "what we proclaim is not ourselves, but Jesus Christ as Lord" (2 Cor 4:5). However, as Zack Eswine points out:

> While the self is not the object of Christian preaching, the self is the instrument through which Christ is preached. Notice Paul's identification of self with instrumentality: "For what we proclaim

2. Hans, "Preaching Through Personal Pain," 97.
3. Day, *Preaching with all You've Got*, 12.

is not ourselves, but Jesus Christ as Lord, *with ourselves as your servants* for Jesus's sake" (2 Cor 4:5, emphasis added). What we preach subordinates and veils our personal stories, but how we preach requires our story. Our story takes the posture of a bond-servant for Jesus's sake.[4]

At times, the prophets' own lives speak to a shared experience with their audience; they demonstrate a transparent vulnerability that shows that the messengers of God's perfect truth are not themselves perfect:

> There is a prophetic vulnerability that is vital to biblical preaching. The prophets can be transparent about their own sin (Isa 6:5), their own humble history (Amos 7:14), their honest questions (Hab 1:2), and their fears (Jer 1:6). Likewise, the prophet's teaching often comes to us in the context of our knowledge of their weakness. Elijah thinks he is alone and wants to die in response to Jezebel's threat. Such personal issues are not hidden from us as we read the prophetic ministry of the Word.[5]

This vulnerability between the preacher and audience can help the preacher to come near in relevance, as discussed in the previous chapter. Haddon Robinson describes how his preaching on God's grace became more impactful during a period in which he was living through deep personal pain: "I had experienced God's grace anew, and the power of that grace simply came through, without my striving for it to happen."[6] At other times, the prophet's own experience is illustrative or analogous to the message he brings. Bullock says that the prophets communicated through speaking, writing, and also through symbolic acts.[7] There are times when symbolic acts or object lessons, and even the genuine experiences of life, communicate alongside our words. Authors and commentators at times refer to symbolic acts and life experiences interchangeably, so to differentiate the two in this chapter I will consider symbolic acts to be those actions or object lessons the prophet is instructed to do in conjunction with a message he is instructed to give. Life experiences are aspects of the prophet's own life which often frame a message and may be something they are commanded to do, but are not explicitly commanded for the purpose of conveying a message.

4. Eswine, *Preaching to a Post-Everything World*, 88.
5. Ibid., 89–90.
6. Robinson, *Making a Difference in Preaching*, 51–53.
7. Bullock, *An Introduction to the Old Testament Prophetic Books*, 231–32.

Part Two

This chapter will highlight several examples of each of these to encourage us as preachers to be aware of ways where life experiences can reinforce our message and where a familiar object lesson can more effectively bring the point home. In the following pages we will consider how the prophets' own experiences were sometimes living examples or "living letters" (2 Cor 3:3) of their message as well as how the prophets were directed by God at times to use imaginative object lessons to portray his truth.

LIVING LETTERS

Perhaps there is no better example of a prophet's own life experience illustrating his message, than the "gut-wrenching real-life drama"[8] of the prophet Hosea's marriage. Hosea's prophetic message opens with his own back story: "When the LORD first spoke through Hosea, the LORD said to Hosea, 'Go, take to yourself a wife of whoredom and have children of whoredom, for the land commits great whoredom by forsaking the Lord.'" (Hos 1:2). As the story continues to unfold, his wife bears three children. The first child is apparently the son of the prophet, "she conceived and bore him a son" (1:3), but the following two children's parentage is in doubt. By the time the third is announced, the child is named, "not my people" (1:9), which might also be heard as Hosea saying the child was "not mine."[9] There is a clear analogy being developed between the children born out of apparent unfaithfulness and the unfaithfulness of Israel to God (1:10; 2:1–23). This biographical sketch closes with the restoration of the prophet's wife (3:1–3), which corresponds to the restoration of Israel in relationship with God (3:4–5). Hosea's own story helps the audience grasp that even in the face of their indefensible unfaithfulness; restoration to God is still possible.

Hosea is also an excellent example of the theological depth that can be understood from personal experience illumined by God's word. My

---

8. Chisholm, *Handbook on the Prophets*, 336. Chisholm provides a concise overview of Hosea 1–3 (336–48) from the perspective of the prophet's real marriage, broken by unfaithfulness but restored by grace. See also Bullock, *An Introduction to the Old Testament Prophetic Books*, 106–10; and Matthews, *The Hebrew Prophets and Their Social World*, 90–93. In contrast, Stuart, *Hosea-Jonah*, 22–68, is more cautious about assuming the details are actually intended to describe the prophet's marriage, separation and remarriage.

9. Matthews, *The Hebrew Prophets and Their Social World*, 91, suggests that the name "not my people" also "suggests that Hosea suspected the child was not actually his, given his wife's unfaithfulness." This would heighten Hosea's personal vulnerability in relating this aspect of the story.

simplified definition of prophetic preaching is: bringing God's past redemptive acts and future promised hope to bear upon the present circumstances of God's people. Walter Brueggemann dares to suggest that in the midst of Hosea's tragic love story, "chapter 2 is among the most important presentations of covenantal theology in all of the Old Testament," and that it is "unmistakable that the completed book of Hosea offers assurance for Israel's survival and well-being beyond the deep dislocation of judgment."[10] Another way to say it is Hosea is incarnational, in that Hosea acts in ways that reveal God's character and also gives voice to God's own emotions (Hos 11:8–9).[11] Some might ask "what kind of God would put his faithful servant through such heartbreak?" but that is the wrong question. Instead, Hosea's life experience is divinely intended to lead us to ask "what kind of love is this that will go so far to bring us back?"

In pastoral ministry I have had the privilege of seeing the kind of reconciliation Hosea depicts lived out in present-day marriages. Hosea's story is the stuff of the real lives of broken people in a broken world. However, there are personal stories that shouldn't be told when confidentiality would be compromised or when it would draw attention away from the message of God's grace to the sinful drama itself. Richard Exley warns us to find the right balance between transparency and "emotional exhibitionism" by suggesting that our own stories should convey hope of victory, rather than ongoing struggle, and should more frequently reveal our own missteps than the mistakes of others.[12] Hosea is a good example of this balance. Gomer's unfaithfulness is evident, but not the focus. The focus is on God's relationship with, and message for, Israel and the trajectory of Hosea's transparency is toward hope and restoration.

Jeremiah is another example of the prophet's marriage situation reinforcing his message. In this case the prophet is forbidden by God to take a wife or raise a family because of the terrible things that will befall wives and children in the coming siege (Jer 16:1–4). Furthermore, Jeremiah is not to join in the grieving of funerals or the celebrations of weddings or other occasions of mirth (16:5–9). During Jeremiah's ministry others carry on with the normal ebb and flow of life, "eating and drinking, marrying and giving in marriage" as they did "until the days when Noah entered the ark" (Matt 24:38). However, Jeremiah is to remain focused on the coming calamity.

---

10. Brueggemann, *An Introduction to the Old Testament*, 247–49.
11. Ibid., 247–50.
12. Exley, "Overexposure," 517–19.

Part Two

Perhaps it is Jeremiah who inspires Paul's call to single-minded singleness in the midst of distressing times (1 Cor 7:25–28). Certainly Jeremiah's example teaches us something about denying one's own temporary comfort and pleasantries for the sake of God's eternal purposes.

In another vignette of Jeremiah's own experience, the Lord directs him to purchase a plot of land and file the title deed in a clay pot at the county courthouse (Jer 32:1–15). Jeremiah seems a little confused about why God would have him buy a field in such dire times, when the Babylonians are about to take Jerusalem. So he does what we should also do when God's way is perplexing: Jeremiah prays. First, in prayer he rehearses God's character and recalls the Lord's faithfulness (Jer 32:16–22). He prayerfully reminds himself of who God is and what he has done. Then he rehearses the present situation, with the looming captivity, which is also God's doing (32:23–24). "Yet you, O Lord God, have said to me, 'Buy the field for money and get witnesses—though the city is given into the hands of the Chaldeans.'" (32:25). Jeremiah is asking, "Why should I buy the field if the Babylonians are about to take it for themselves?"

In response to the obedient and yet perplexed prophet, God explained this object lesson of hope. The Lord uses Jeremiah's own words, "Is anything too hard for me?" (32:26, cp. 32:17), to remind Jeremiah that God would do what seemed impossible. All of God's word would be fulfilled. The Chaldeans would purge Jerusalem (32:28–35), but they would not keep it (32:36–41). In this lesson of hope in the midst of despair, the Lord gives the first mention through Jeremiah of the new and everlasting covenant (32:40), and he assures that fields will again be bought and sold and title deeds signed and witnessed and recorded in clay pots at the county courthouse (32:42–44). Jeremiah exemplifies in his own life the message God intends to convey through him.

In the final days before Jerusalem's fall, and in the turmoil which followed, Jeremiah's proclamations decrease and his life and experiences "become the message—a dual message about a suffering nation and a suffering God in whose service Jeremiah remained steadfast to the very end."[13] Both by his words and in the hardships he endures, Jeremiah declares something about the suffering servant, the premier prophet who was to come, who would also be willing to suffer for his rebellious people. If the book of Lamentations is written by Jeremiah as the Septuagint version suggests, the record of the prophet's own laments are also a significant pastoral mes-

---

13. Lundbom, *The Hebrew Prophets*, 218.

sage of grief and hope. The prophet's own experience of grief is a prophetic message to others.

The example of the prophet Jonah takes the principle of an authentic message being supported by one's life experience in a different direction. We expect to see the prophets as our heroes, and yet we should also know that they, like preachers today, are imperfect men "with a nature like ours" (Jas 5:17). Perhaps Jonah had heard Haddon Robinson's advice: "Congregations dislike first-person stories when the preacher emerges regularly as the hero."[14] Jonah is clearly not the hero in his story. Ironically, Jonah's story isn't so much about Jonah or Nineveh at all. Jonah's story is about God's sovereignty and his mercy, and about Israel and how they were to show the glory of God's mercies to the nations. Jonah's lack of care or concern for the evil and unrighteous pagans around him was representative of a similar mindset shared by all of Israel.[15] It continues to have the same force today. While we are amused by the continual irony in the book of Jonah, we ought to be convicted by similar attitudes hidden away in our own hearts. The true mastery of Jonah is how the prophet, in his own story, so perfectly exposes the prejudices of his audience. The story of Jonah's own wrestling with God is an effective way to slip the message past the audience's defenses and into their hearts. In the same way, when a preacher today tells of a time when his own desires collided with God's will, it helps the audience to acknowledge the same tendency in themselves.

In these examples the prophets demonstrate that effective preaching can be greatly assisted when the life experience of the preacher embodies the message. If we assume that this narrative framing of the prophet's message with the prophet's story is intentional, then we should be encouraged to look for ways that the Lord will use our life experience to frame his message through us. For example, my life experiences as a missionary have strengthened my messages to our church concerning the mission we have in our community. Similarly, a pastor who is active and effective in personal evangelism will more effectively exhort the church to witness because his life and character model the message. We must also be aware that this framing of the message with the life of the messenger occurs whether we intend it to or not, so we should be careful that we live in the gospel we preach.

"Living in the gospel" may occur in a case similar to Hosea, where the preacher exemplifies forgiveness and mercy—mercy given, or even better

14. Robinson, *Biblical Preaching*, 160.
15. Clendenen, "Textlinguistics and Prophecy in the Book of the Twelve," 398.

mercy received. It could be similar to Jeremiah, where the preacher has endured hardship for the sake of the gospel. It might also be that our own cultivated prayer life which expresses grief, hope and faith will strengthen, even unintentionally, our spiritual shepherding of the church. Finally, like the example of Jonah, the stories we tell on ourselves will illustrate things our listeners need to learn about themselves. The prophet's use of their own stories suggests to us that we too must be ready to share "not only the gospel of God but also our own lives" (1 Thess 2:8, NET).

This sharing of our own lives is more than being good examples for others to emulate. Our churches also need leaders who trust in the gospel enough themselves that they don't need to guard their own image. While we don't ever want to glorify sin or make it seemingly more excusable by stories of our own failings, we do at times need to admit to our own failings if we are going to demonstrate our trust in God's grace. Care must be given that we don't spoil the example and hope of victory over sin that a congregation needs to see in their shepherd's life. Joe Stowell warns that "Indiscriminate revelation may diminish our greatest ministry, that of cutting a godly wake by the example of our own lives."[16] Still, the godly wake must also include ripples of confession and forgiveness if it is to be authentic and helpful. Stowell demonstrates this balance by pointing out that Paul exhorts Timothy to be an example in speech, conduct, love, faith and purity (1 Tim 4:12–15), but he does not expect Timothy to be perfect in these attributes. Instead, others would see Timothy's progress as he grows in God's grace.

OBJECT LESSONS

A similar, but perhaps more intriguing and intimidating aspect of the prophets' preaching, is their use of object lessons. Their object lessons are intriguing because they captivate our attention and linger in our memories. They are intimidating because some of these object lessons are the kind of things we pray the Lord would never ask us to do. Object lessons differ from life experiences in that these are symbolic acts or dramatic ploys the prophets are instructed to enact in order to convey their message. The act or ploy itself is intended to convey meaning.[17]

---

16. Stowell, "Self-Disclosure that Glorifies Christ," 143.
17. Caird, *The Language and Imagery of the Bible*, 22–23.

For example, Isaiah is instructed to walk around lightly dressed and barefoot for three years (Isa 20:1–2).[18] When things are going well we might say that we are "living the dream," but Isaiah is living the classic dream people may have when they harbor anxiety or fear exposure: a dream where one is underdressed in public. His dramatic act symbolizes the humiliation his message predicts for Egypt and Cush, as well as for those in Judah who trust in these nations instead of trusting in the Lord (20:3–6).

Jeremiah often uses dramatic acts or object lessons: "Jeremiah's message contains more than words. Like prophets before him (e.g. Isa 20; Hos 1–3), he dramatized God's spoken word with symbolic actions. In this way, Jeremiah's life became a living embodiment and a metaphor of what was about to happen."[19] For example, Jeremiah purchases a loincloth, wears it for a while and then stashes it among the rocks along the river. There the loincloth is ruined (Jer 13:1–7). The object lesson is intended to convey that as long as the people clung to the Lord like the loincloth clinging to a man's hips, they could fulfill their created purpose, but when they departed to where they did not belong, they were ruined and unfit for God's use (13:8–11).

On another occasion Jeremiah is instructed to go and buy a pottery flask, and then go to his preaching place, where he will smash the flask in the midst of his message, in order to underscore the word of the Lord: "So will I break this people and this city, as one breaks a potter's vessel" (Jer 19:1–13). The dramatic act would have been unexpected and memorable, which gave his audience reason to remember the message behind that act. Perhaps they would say among themselves, "Remember when Jeremiah smashed that flask and everybody jumped?" "Yeah, I remember that . . . why did he do that? Oh, that's right; he said that 'God was going to smash us and Jerusalem in the same way!'"

Jeremiah's broken flask reminds me of another broken bottle. While preaching from Mark chapter 14, I was describing the scene where the woman broke open the bottle of costly perfume that could not be re-sealed—it would all be expended. I had prepared a ceramic flask to hold up as I talked about this costly ointment which she had brought, and at one point I unexpectedly struck the neck of the flask against a hard object, breaking it open.

---

18. Chisholm, *Handbook on the Prophets*, 60, points out that while the Hebrew word used in Isaiah 20:2 can at times mean "naked'" in this case it likely means "stripped of outer garments" as the first half of the verse suggests.

19. Lessing, *Prepare the Way*, 400. See also Lundbom, *The Hebrew Prophets*, 213–15.

Part Two

I had everyone's attention. "Break the bottle" became shorthand for "hold nothing back, pour it all out, serve the Lord extravagantly."

Similar to symbolic action is Jeremiah's use of a dramatic ploy, a "tactic for redefining a situation contrary to general expectations, and therefore effective in catching the other players off-guard."[20] It is American football's double-reverse or faked punt applied to a speaking situation. Jeremiah approaches the leaders of a clan, the Rechabites, to meet with him in a special room at the temple. Once they are all gathered, with others from the Jerusalem establishment also apparently present, Jeremiah sets wine before them, and offers them a drink. Perhaps those observing smirk to themselves, because everyone knows that the Rechabites adhere to their father's command never to drink wine (among other restrictions), and Jeremiah has just made a grave social *faux pas*. Jeremiah seems to be inviting them to violate their vow and it appears Jeremiah's public authority will be diminished if they refuse to do so, as the observers likely expect. The Rechabites graciously but firmly refuse Jeremiah's invitation, but rather than diminish his status, their refusal gives him a platform. He then preaches to all the people: the Rechabites keep the commands of their father, but Judah does not keep the commands of God (Jer 35:1–19). The Jerusalem establishment never saw his surprise twist coming, so it more easily penetrated their defenses against listening to what Jeremiah had to say.

Guinness remarks on the effectiveness of the ploy, as compared to merely declaring Jerusalem's failing:

> Doubtless, the citizens of Jerusalem slunk away rapidly that day, but the turning of the tables was deeper and longer lasting than that. They would never be able to see a Rechabite out in the streets or in the marketplace without being reminded that these people had called them into question. The despised fundamentalists [the Rechabites] were a living rebuke to their faithlessness.[21]

None of the prophets employ symbolic acts as much as Ezekiel, who "virtually made it into a prophetic art."[22] Some have pointed out that in modern society Ezekiel's symbolic acts would likely be considered as evidence of mental illness.[23] Preachers should feel free to emulate Ezekiel's

---

20. Guinness, *Fool's Talk*, 166.
21. Ibid., 166.
22. Bullock, *Introduction to the Old Testament Prophetic Books*, 282–83.
23. Gunkel, "The Israelite Prophecy from the Time of Amos," 52.

willingness to extend beyond the expected in order to communicate effectively, without feeling obligated to exactly imitate his actions.

Ezekiel's symbolic actions include being confined to his house and being mute for a period of time (Ezek 3:22–27). His symbols of the coming siege include building a model of the city under siege (4:1–3), eating limited and unclean rations (4:9–17), and a prophetic haircut and dramatic siege enactment that prefigures the coming horrors (5:1–12). Later he is commanded to pack his bags, dig a hole through his wall and go out of his house into symbolic captivity in the sight of all the people (12:1–8). These actions are intended to cause people to ask him, "What are you doing?" (12:9). Their queries open the way for the Lord's answer: these actions depict the coming exile and also portray King Zedekiah's futile attempt to escape God's judgment (12:10–16).

Ezekiel also dramatically eats his food with quaking and groaning (12:17–20), he groans aloud, so that they will ask what he is groaning about (21:1–7), and then he commences an imaginary sword fight portraying the violent conclusion of Babylon's siege (21:8–32). On a brighter note, he later takes two sticks and identifies them with Judah and Israel, then joins them together into one, showing how the divided kingdom will again be reunited when God restores them by bringing life from death (Ezek 37:15–28). This last object lesson also highlights the importance of understanding how the prophets use object lessons and explain them. Ezekiel's object lesson with the two sticks has been consistently and significantly misused by the Mormon sect to represent their additional writings being joined to the Bible. However, such an interpretation is shown to be completely fanciful in light of Ezekiel's own explanation of what the object lesson means.

Repeatedly, Ezekiel's object lessons are shown to provoke questions and incite interest, as well as making the explanation more memorable. It is worth noting that Ezekiel uses consistent language between his symbolic acts and his main point. As Chapell says concerning illustrations, we should "rain the key words"[24] of the object lesson into the explanation. If it is true that people often remember the illustration even if they forget the point, they will remember an object lesson or symbolic act even more. And, if the object lesson is well chosen and well connected to the truth being proclaimed, it will help the point, and not just the object lesson, to be remembered.

---

24. Chapell, *Christ-Centered Preaching*, 197.

Part Two

A few years ago I began doing a brief "Kid's Talk" with younger children before they were dismissed to a lesson time during my sermon. Encouraged by the prophets' example, I often use an object lesson to make a simple point for the kids that also leads into my sermon. While I tell everyone that this is for the kids, really it's for the entire congregation—but let's keep that our secret. My sermon introduction or content within the sermon will return to that opening object lesson. I vary the approach: sometimes the link is obvious, other times it is more subtle. This has become an effective way to communicate truth to the kids, to gain the interest of adults, and also to foster family conversations about the sermon following the service.

Object lessons or dramatic ploys can also be used within our sermons. Many churches have effectively used the nailing of confessions to a wooden cross to drive home the attachment of our own sins to Jesus's substitutionary death. One year in a mid-day Good Friday service I took that dramatic object lesson one step further. Toward the end of the service we removed all of the notes of confession from the cross and ran them through a paper shredder. This had the dual effect of assuring the participants that their confessed sins were truly eradicated, neither I nor anyone else would read them after the service. In addition, every time they heard the common sound of a paper shredder it would remind them of how their sins were forever removed in Jesus, never to be brought up against them.

An example of an object lesson that served my purpose at multiple levels was one I used while on furlough during our service with a missionary radio ministry. My text was "Him [Jesus] we preach . . . according to his power which works in us" Col 1:28–29. I had emphasized that the power of our mission's message was the gospel of Christ, not the kilowatts of our transmitters, and that we served by Christ's grace and enablement. As a closing illustration I showed a small, solar-powered, fixed-frequency radio receiver like the ones we distributed to listeners in rural areas. This radio could not be used to listen to any other radio station except our gospel programs. I used this solar-powered radio as a visible metaphor of our ministry, "powered by the Son to proclaim God's word." Three years later, on my next furlough visit, people still remembered that sun-powered radio that was dedicated to proclaiming the gospel.

Kelli Worral points out that some may hesitate to use dramatic ploys or object lessons because such techniques are associated with "contemporary" or "seeker sensitive" circles and might seem to be merely "resorting to entertainment."²⁵ Worral gives a nice summary of how drama and object lessons have been used since the beginning of biblical worship. For example, God uses an unforgettable dramatic ploy involving the offering of Isaac to speak to Abraham (and us) about faith (Gen 22). The feasts of Israel dramatically remind Israel of what God has done and will do (Lev 27). Every Old Testament sacrifice is an object lesson concerning sin and the fall and the need for a substitute. The prophets of Israel are simply carrying on a tradition deeply rooted in the Old Testament and continued into the New Testament, as is seen in Jesus's numerous object lessons. God's penchant for object lessons continues in the ordinances of baptism (Rom 6:1–4) and the Lord's table (1 Cor 11:23–26). Making intentional use of object lessons and ploys is not capitulating to contemporary culture, it is joining God in how he communicates.

The prophets spoke well; they spoke boldly, and they also supplemented their words with symbolic acts and their own life experiences which embodied their message. The prophets are a provocative example to us to remember that our communication of God's word is both verbal and nonverbal. This is also evident in Paul's words to the Philippians: "What you have learned and received and *heard and seen in me*—practice these things, and the God of peace will be with you" (Phil 4:9). May the Spirit of God guide us, as he did his prophets, so that what our audience hears us say is effectively reinforced by what they see in us and what they see us do.

---

25. Worral, "Drama and the Sermon," 295–96.

10

Continuing to Preach like the Prophets

As an example of suffering and patience, brothers,
take the prophets who spoke in the name of the Lord.
JAMES 5:10

The prophets' faithfulness to God's calling sets an example
to all who desire to proclaim God's word today.
GARY SMITH[1]

The prophets are encouraging examples in how they preach. They are also encouraging examples in how they continue to preach. They keep going; they don't stop; they don't give up. The prophets often preached in difficult circumstances, to an apathetic audience, with a discouraging lack of response. What is even more noteworthy in their persistence is that many of them were warned in advance that they were being sent to a people who would not hear, yet still they preached. It is hard to persist and give something your all, when you are warned in advance that your efforts must ultimately fail. Yet, at times, this is our lot as preachers. We are to preach "in season and out of season" when people will "not endure sound teaching" but will "turn away from listening to the truth and wander off into myths" (2 Tim 4:2–4). Even when fruitfulness seems out of season, faithfulness must continue.

---

1. Smith, *The Prophets as Preachers*, 1.

Continuing to Preach like the Prophets

Zack Eswine describes the situation preachers and prophets sometimes face:

> The faithful preacher may also face long seasons of winter with little accompanying warmth. The reason for this fact resides in the nature of the preacher's audience. Like Ezekiel, the preacher may have to faithfully speak God's words "whether they hear or refuse" (Ezek 2:7). Like Timothy, far from finding other more attractive methods of communication, he will need to hang in there and continue to "preach the word" even while some people "will not endure sound teaching" and "will turn away from listening to the truth" (2 Tim 4:2–4).[2]

Certainly the prophets experienced fruitful times of significant response, such as the years of revival during the reigns of Hezekiah and Josiah and when the people listened to Haggai and rose up to build (Hag 1:12–14). However, much of the prophets' preaching seems to occur out of season, when fruit not only is not evident, it is not expected. For example, when Isaiah is called to preach, a call that has reverberated in the hearts of thousands of servants since, we prefer to forget the words which next come from the Lord who commissions him: "Go and say to this people: 'Keep on hearing, but do not understand; keep on seeing, but do not perceive'" (Isa 6:9). In the very next chapter,[3] the prophet sees this dire prediction confirmed when the newly installed young king Ahaz refuses to heed God's word from God's messenger (Isa 7:1–17).

At the other end of Isaiah's ministry, or at least the other end of the book of Isaiah, the prophet summarizes the lack of fruitful response to God's word from his preaching: "when I called you did not answer; when I spoke you did not listen" (Isa 65:13). Isaiah is not unique in this regard; rejection was a common occupational hazard of the preaching prophets. Yet, though they were rejected, they still faithfully fulfilled their ministry. Faithfulness is one more lesson we can learn from the preaching of the prophets. Just as we can learn from the rhetoric of the prophets, we must also learn from their resilience. We need to take their persistence to heart because preaching can be at times a discouraging business. Many discouraged preachers, lacking visible results, have privately appropriated Paul's

---

2. Eswine, *Preaching to a Post-Everything World*, 248.

3. The events of Isaiah chapter 7 occur approximately 5 years after Isaiah's call (Chisholm, *Handbook on the Prophets*, 28). These chapters in Isaiah are arranged rhetorically rather than in tight chronology, thus Ahaz's refusal to heed God's prophet is emblematic of the spiritual dullness of Judah during Isaiah's ministry (Isa 6:9–10).

Part Two

classic quote from Isaiah 65:2, "All day long I have held out my hands to a disobedient and contrary people" (Rom 10:21). Later, in the same letter, Paul provides a framework for persistence: "Rejoice in hope, be patient in tribulation, be constant in prayer" (Rom 12:12). These three phrases offer a helpful template for these concluding pages, which will seek to highlight some encouragement for preachers from the persistence of the prophets.

REJOICING IN HOPE

Jeremiah is an obvious example of a stubbornly persistent prophet. Like Isaiah, he is told by the Lord that the people will not listen to him: "So you shall speak all these words to them, but they will not listen to you. You shall call to them, but they will not answer you" (Jer 7:27). Jeremiah is put in the stocks because of his preaching (Jer 20:1–2). He is falsely accused and imprisoned in a brutal dungeon (37:11–20) and later cast into a cistern where his enemies intended to leave him to die (Jer 38:1–9). In this later case, he is arrested specifically because his preaching does not agree with the political narrative of the day. Even though the king knows that Jeremiah is a faithful prophet of the Lord and his words are true, the king does not publicly protect him from the politically correct mob.

Jeremiah is not simply a boundless optimist who determines to respond in joy to every situation. No, he is closer to how James describes Elijah, "a man with a nature like ours" (Jas 5:17). In the midst of the troubles which come upon the people, Jeremiah is burdened and joins in their grief: "Oh that my head were waters, and my eyes a fountain of tears, that I might weep day and night for the slain of the daughter of my people!" (Jer 9:1). When he is released from his sentence in the stocks, he boldly proclaims God's righteous judgment upon his tormentor, but he sounds somewhat broken in his complaint to the Lord:

> O Lord, you have deceived me,
> and I was deceived;
> you are stronger than I,
> and you have prevailed.
> I have become a laughingstock all the day;
> everyone mocks me.
> For whenever I speak, I cry out,
> I shout, "Violence and destruction!"

> For the word of the Lord has become for me
> a reproach and derision all day long.
> If I say, "I will not mention him,
> or speak any more in his name,"
> there is in my heart as it were a burning fire
> shut up in my bones,
> and I am weary with holding it in,
> and I cannot (Jer 20:7–9).

While most of us have not "resisted to the point of shedding your blood" (Heb 12:4), as could be said of Jeremiah, perhaps we may identify at times with the competing realities of divine compulsion and despair in difficulties. Jeremiah feels let down by God, and he would resign his pulpit if he could, but as Paul says, "necessity is laid upon me. Woe to me if I do not preach the gospel" (1 Cor 9:16). Still, it is more than mere obligation or duty which keeps Jeremiah going. His contemplation continues in Jeremiah 20:11–13, where we hear the prophet's hope:

> But the Lord is with me as a dread warrior;
> therefore my persecutors will stumble;
> they will not overcome me.
> They will be greatly shamed,
> for they will not succeed.
> Their eternal dishonor
> will never be forgotten.
> O Lord of hosts, who tests the righteous,
> who sees the heart and the mind,
> let me see your vengeance upon them,
> for to you have I committed my cause.
> Sing to the Lord;
> praise the Lord!
> For he has delivered the life of the needy
> from the hand of evildoers (Jer 20:11–13).

Jeremiah sees and deeply grieves the broken present reality, but he also sees a greater reality and an alternative future. As a true prophet he is able to remain steadfast in the face of present despair, in the light of the Lord's past redemption and future hope. Brueggemann warns us to not allow the apparent futility we experience in our present impossible circumstances to steal away our hope in the certain reality of God's promised future: "the fundamental distinction between social prospect and divine promise is crucial. We need to be saying to each other that our energies are rooted in and aimed toward God's promises and not social prospects."[4]

The "Book of Lamentations"[5] gives evidence that the prophet grieves the hopelessness of the present, while also continuing in hope because "the steadfast love of the LORD never ceases; his mercies never come to an end; they are new every morning; great is your faithfulness" (Lam 3:22–23). An even more illumining line is the one that follows these. Having lost everything, Jeremiah has not lost hope because, "'The LORD is my portion,' says my soul, therefore I will hope in him" (Lam 3:24). Jeremiah's hope is not in present prosperity, assured success or immediate deliverance from troubles; his spirit hungers for, and is sustained by, the Lord himself.

Looking more carefully into Jeremiah's prayers, we can discern that Jeremiah's hope is fueled by God's word. The mocking he endures (20:7) is expressed in the language of Psalm 22:7. His compulsion to continue to preach (20:9) echoes the words of Job (Job 32:18–20) and David (Psalm 39:2–3). In the midst of his suffering, Jeremiah's hope is in the Lord whom he knows "tests the righteous" (compare Psalm 11:5) and who "hears the needy and does not despise his own people who are prisoners" (compare Psalm 69:33).

Jeremiah's allusions to Scripture show that when they are hard-pressed, these persistent prophets are upheld by God's truth. They base their prayers on what they know from God's word about his character and promises. Jeremiah bases his hope in part on truth about God from David's Psalms. Similarly, Daniel's prayer is explicitly informed by Jeremiah's prophecy (Dan 9:2). Habakkuk's prayer leans on the Lord who redeemed Israel out of Egypt, brought them through the wilderness, and can be trusted to fulfill his word (Hab 3:1–19). Habakkuk's prayer is filled with allusions to historical scriptures. Then, in the conclusion of his prayer, he appropriates the song of David, "He made my feet like the feet of a deer and set me secure on the heights"(2 Sam 22:34; cp. Hab 3:19) which David spoke "on the day when the LORD delivered him from the hand of all his enemies"

---

4. Brueggemann and Miller, *Like Fire in the Bones*, 182.

5. The authorship of Lamentations is anonymous, although tradition and the Septuagint ascribe the book to Jeremiah. Thus, I am treating the prayers of Lamentations as those of Jeremiah or another from the era of, and with the perspective of, Jeremiah. See House, *Lamentations*, 283–302 for an extended discussion of the authorship of Lamentations.

(2 Sam 22:1). Habakkuk is declaring that just as the Lord delivered David, he will be faithful to continue to deliver his people from all their enemies. The prayers which strengthen these persistent prophets are not merely the requests for what they choose to believe that God will do. Their prayers are firmly rooted in the previously revealed character and promises of God.

I have often used specific prayers from God's word to pray for our church and even to lead the church in prayer. I believe this is a good way to help the church to pray in accordance to God's will, and to teach the church how to pray. However, the way that these prophets include allusion to God's word in their prayers, rather than specific quotations, suggests something deeper. Perhaps these allusions indicate that these prophets have so filled themselves with God's word that when they are pressed, God's previously revealed truth leaks out of them in their prayers. In the course of their life and ministry they have regularly fed their souls on God's word and they know his name, his character. When their faith is tested by troubling circumstances the truth of God which has been treasured away in their hearts now fuels their faith and its echoes are evident in their heartfelt pleadings and prayers. We need to likewise feed our souls consistently on God's truth so that in difficult times it can feed our faith.

PATIENT IN TRIBULATION

Like Isaiah and Jeremiah, Ezekiel is also sent to preach to Israel "whether they hear or refuse to hear," but he is also exhorted, "be not afraid of them, nor be afraid of their words ... nor be dismayed by their looks" (Ezek 2:3–7). These exhortations suggest that Ezekiel would meet antagonistic opposition from his audience. He would have reason to fear, and so God says, "do not be afraid of them." They will speak violently against him, perhaps calling him a hater and a traitor, and so he is told, "do not be afraid of their words." They will look at him with disdain, with anger, or perhaps with elitist indifference, and so he is told, "do not be dismayed by their looks." We also preach in an age where good is called evil, truth is forbidden to be spoken in many public arenas, and faithful preaching may bring retaliation rather than appreciation. Frequently those who dare to proclaim God's unchanging truth are derided as haters or dismissed as irrelevant. We need to know how Ezekiel remained faithful in a faithless age.

Ezekiel is not to measure his ministry by the response of the people, but by his faithfulness as the Lord's messenger. He is not to give into the temptation to lighten his touch or soften his rhetoric in order to gain a more favorable reception. Ezekiel is a dynamic messenger; his rhetorical phrasing remains in our vernacular over 2500 years later. He communicates and demonstrates his messages in dramatic attention getting ways. Still, the measure of Ezekiel's ministry is not in results, but in his faithfulness to God's call, as is made clear in the analogy of the watchman (Ezek 3:16–21; 33:2–9). Faithful watchmen must continue to watch and warn even when the prevailing winds blow stiffly against them.

Surveying a few more of these persistent prophets, we are reminded that Hosea persists through the heartbreak and grief in a marriage "made in heaven," but broken in pieces in real life (Hos 1:2–3). Amos is falsely accused of treason and conspiracy by the priest Amaziah, who puts words in his mouth against the king's life (Amos 7:10–13). This same opponent is also apparently "insinuating that Amos [only] preached at Bethel because the remuneration was better there than in Judah."[6]

Preachers today must expect to face similar adversity. There are times when our own families and those dearest to us will be caught in the immoral currents of the day. The hurt will eat at our own soul even as some adversaries will see in the crisis an opportunity to impugn our credibility or label us hypocrites. Pastors were once respected leaders and opinion shapers in their communities, but now we may be openly mocked and our motives maligned. We will at times be labelled "haters" for failing to embrace the current social agenda, even while we give ourselves in love to show and tell the gospel of the one who gave himself in love for us all. How can we continue in these personal tribulations of the prophetic preacher?

Habakkuk persists in trusting the Lord even when the word of the Lord makes it clear that great trouble and difficult times are coming upon Judah and therefore also upon the prophet. He determines that even when all temporal prosperity is taken away, "yet I will rejoice in the Lord; I will take joy in the God of my salvation." (Hab 3:18). In fact, in Habakkuk's dialog with the Lord, his "honest-to-God" prayer points to another important factor in the prophets' perseverance.

PERSEVERING IN PRAYER

The prophets continue in hope, patiently enduring opposition because they "continue steadfastly in prayer" (Col 4:2). For example, one of the first

6. Stuart, *Hosea-Jonah*, 376.

things we learn about the prophet Daniel is his personal faithful devotion to the Lord. Even when he is taken into exile as a young man and enrolled in the University of Babylon, he continues to live out that personal devotion (Dan 1:8). Soon after, when events conspire to threaten Daniel and his friends, along with all the wise men of Babylon, Daniel calls a prayer meeting with his friends to seek mercy from God, and then rejoices in prayer when God answers them (Dan 2:17-22). Even when his later opponents make Daniel's prayers to the Lord illegal, he continues steadfastly in prayer (Dan 6:3-15).

We have benefited in multiple ways from Daniel's persistence in prayer. First, one of his prayers results in God providing a timetable for the restoration of all things which has fortified believers' hope for the last 2500 years (9:20-27). Daniel's prayers strengthen his own soul in difficult times, and God's specific answer to his prayer still strengthens us today. Daniel's experience shows us that our faithful God's answer to the persistent preacher's prayer can have a long range impact. Our own steadfastness in prayer through difficult circumstances will both vitalize our ministry and also enable us to share God's hope with those to whom we are entrusted to minister.

On the other hand, if we don't follow the prophets' example of perseverance in prayer, it can diminish our ministry. There have been times when I experienced a weight of tribulations and a seeming silence from heaven, and I withdrew from prayer instead of persevering in it. The result was a spiraling down of spiritual vitality which also impacted my ministry. The antidote was grieving openly to God in prayer and focusing my prayer on God's character and his promised redemption, rather than focusing on the circumstances.

This is what we see in the prayers that Daniel, Jeremiah and Habakkuk pray in the midst of opposition. Each of these men are found in authentic and open prayer to God, because the psalmist has taught them to "trust in him at all times, O people; pour out your heart before him; God is a refuge for us" (Psalm 62:8). Their prayers are not empty repetitions or a pretense of confidence. They pour out their hearts to God; they describe the present reality as they see it, in unguarded authenticity. And in one example that we are allowed to overhear, the largest part of Daniel's prayer is given to honest and contrite confession of the sins of his people, identifying himself with them (9:4-15).

This open authenticity in prayer is heard when Habakkuk bares his soul as he dares to enter into a disputation with God over the use of Babylon as God's agent to chasten Israel (Hab 1:12—2:1). Jeremiah's prayer describes his trouble and those who are against him in devastating detail (20:7–10), and yet he expresses hope in the Lord and his coming victory (20:11–13). But this future hope doesn't change the situation today; exile is still before them, Jerusalem will still be ravished, and multitudes will die. Jeremiah's prayer acknowledges the despair in his heart (20:14–18).

This stubborn determination to assert the critical reality of the present and to voice genuine grief over it is necessary if despair is to be answered by hope.[7] Too often we put the most optimistic spin on the present, "assuming" the best instead of "believing" something worse, which God has in fact declared. But, if we assume something better than God's assessment, we may suppress legitimate grief that should be expressed for the present brokenness and in so doing, leave no room or hunger for God's hope. Hope is intended by God to be an answer to our despair, but blind optimism has no need of God's hope. Instead, we need to face reality and grieve the present brokenness in our prayers and in our proclamations. As Russell Moore has said, "We are a prophetic minority who must speak into a world that is . . . exactly what Jesus promised us the world must be."[8] Because of the hatred of the world for God, our vulnerability in the world, and the prophetic mission given to us, Jesus also prayed for us:

> I have given them your word, and the world has hated them because they are not of the world, just as I am not of the world. I do not ask that you take them out of the world, but that you keep them from the evil one. They are not of the world, just as I am not of the world. Sanctify them in the truth; your word is truth. As you sent me into the world, so I have sent them into the world. And for their sake I consecrate myself, that they also may be sanctified in truth. (John 17:14–19).

Jesus does not pray for our escape from the hostility of the world, but for our faithful endurance in the midst of that hostility. Jesus's prayer for us, in the midst of the severest test in his own ministry, reminds us of the importance of prayer for persistence in ministry. We must devote ourselves to prayer for the Lord's blessing on our ministry, and we must open our hearts to God in prayer when present trials veil his blessing from our sight.

---

7. See Brueggemann, *Reality, Grief, Hope*, 1–2.
8. Bailey, "Moore on the Margins," 30.

Continuing to Preach like the Prophets

Persevering in prayer is foundational to patiently enduring tribulation and rejoicing in hope.

It may sound trite (and far too alliterated), but it is by praying like the prophets that we will persevere like the prophets in preaching like the prophets. Prayer is not only essential for the fruitfulness of our preaching ministry, but for our protection from discouragement or distraction. Perhaps this is why the Apostles, when a potential conflict was brewing in the growing Jerusalem church, declared: "We must devote ourselves to prayer and to the ministry of the word" (Acts 6:5).

Difficulties and conflicts can discourage us from the ministry of God's word, and success and its accompanying busyness can also lead us astray. Thus Bryan Chapell warns:

> Public ministry true to God's purposes requires devoted private prayer. We should not expect our words to acquaint others with the power of the Spirit if we have not met with him. Faithful preachers plead for God to work as well as for their own accuracy, integrity, and skill in proclaiming his Word. Success in the pulpit can be the force that leads a preacher from prayerful dependence on the Spirit. Congregational accolades for pulpit excellence may tempt one to put too much confidence in personal gifts, acquired skills, or a particular method of preaching. Succumbing to such a temptation is evidenced not so much by a change in belief as by a change in practice. Neglect of prayer signals serious deficiencies in a ministry even if other signs of success have not diminished. We must always remember that popular acclaim is not necessarily the same as spiritual effectiveness.[9]

Still, there is much that pulls at the preaching pastor. There will always be people to visit, phone calls to make, emails to answer, administration to manage, staff to lead and encourage, printed and visual presentations to prepare, and always more studying, outlining, and sermon sharpening to be done. We can easily identify with Azurdia's confession: "Like all hard-working pastors, if I pray only when people and circumstances allow it to be convenient, I would rarely pray." So what shall we do? Azurdia and others suggest blocking out scheduled time to read devotionally and pray.[10] But still, even disciplined time can become dry and routine, going through the motions. Perhaps in those times we can do what some of the prophets

---

9. Chapell, *Christ-Centered Preaching*, 33.
10. Azurdia, *Spirit Empowered Preaching*, 137.

seem to have done, since the words of the Psalms seem to echo inside them. Withdraw to a quiet place, open God's word, especially the Psalms, and read and pray through God's word like those who have gone before us.[11]

LIKE THE PROPHETS

We stand on the shoulders of giants, continuing the ministry of God's messengers, which was practiced before us by our prophetic predecessors. God has given to us the privilege of bringing redemption in Jesus and the hope of his coming to bear upon broken present realities by the power of the Holy Spirit. Such a glorious ministry is worthy of our greatest efforts, even though we know that those greatest efforts will be in vain apart from the effectual working of God's Spirit. The prophets, by the inspiration of the Spirit, grabbed their audiences' attention and proclaimed their message in artfully crafted and insightfully effective ways. They were both clear and persuasive; they got to the point and into people lives. They were able to relate the truth of God to the stuff of real life and through their own lives. They kept at it.

The encouraging example of the preaching of the prophets leads me to pray for our own prophetic preaching. Lord, as insufficient as we are, we ask you to use us as your messengers of redemption and hope in Christ. Fill us with your Spirit so that we may boldly preach and effectively gain a hearing. Use us to clearly and persuasively proclaim your truth in this day to these people for their good and for your glory. Strengthen us when opposition abounds, lift us when our spirits fail and protect us from presumption when you give the increase. Give us fruit that will endure, and guide our own hearts ever closer to you.

---

11. See Whitney, *Praying the Bible*.

Epilogue

A few years ago I had the opportunity to attend a conference at which Dr. Walter Kaiser was speaking. Addressing a room full of preachers, Dr. Kaiser had chosen a text from Isaiah for which many of those in the audience held a contrary eschatological perspective. Pleasantly and persuasively, with winsomeness and wit the good doctor won his way into our hearts and into our heads. I was grateful for the truth he proclaimed to us, but I was even more grateful for what I learned from the way he proclaimed it. He demonstrated how to carefully, convincingly, and uncompromisingly declare God's truth. I learned not only from what this prophetic preacher said, but also from how he said it.

In a similar way, it is my sincere hope that preaching pastors and students of preaching will find this work to be a helpful catalyst and encouragement to read and hear the prophets as preachers. My goal has been that we will continue to learn not only from what the prophets have to say, but how they say it. As we listen to the prophets we will notice different rhetorical strategies among them, as well as how a prophet varies his proclamation in different situations. They will not give us an exact model—preach like this—but they do model an inspired intentionality in how they preach. May we do the same—may you too preach like the prophets, proclaiming God's word of redemption and hope by the power of his Spirit.

Bibliography

Aristotle. *Rhetoric*. W. Rhys Roberts, and W. D. Ross, trans. New York: Cosimo Classics, 2010.
Arndt, William F., et al. *A Greek-English Lexicon of the New Testament and Other Early Christian Literature: A Translation and Adaption of the Fourth Revised and Augmented Edition of Walter Bauer's Griechisch-Deutsches Worterbuch Zu Den Schrift En Des Neuen Testaments Und Der Ubrigen Urchristlichen Literatur*. Chicago: University of Chicago Press, 1996.
Ayer, William Ward. "Pulpit Prophet." *Bibliotheca Sacra* 124, no. 496 (1967) 291–302.
Azurdia, Arturo G. *Spirit Empowered Preaching: Involving the Holy Spirit in Your Ministry*. Fearn: Mentor, 2003.
Bacon, Ernest W. *Spurgeon: Heir of the Puritans*. Arlington Heights, IL: Christian Liberty, 1996.
Bailey, Sarah Pulliam. "Moore on the Margins." *Christianity Today* 59, no. 7 (2015) 30–39.
Barclay, William. *A Spiritual Biography*. Grand Rapids: Eerdmans, 1975.
Barton, John. "Ethics in Isaiah of Jerusalem." In *This Place is Too Small for Us: The Israelite Prophets in Recent Scholarship*, edited by Robert P. Gordon, 80–97. Winona Lake, IN: Eisenbrauns, 1995.
———. *Oracles of God: Perceptions of Ancient Prophecy in Israel After the Exile*. New York: Oxford University Press, 1988.
Ben Zvi, Ehud. "Introduction: Writings, Speeches, and the Prophetic Books: Setting an Agenda." In *Writings and Speech in Israelite and Ancient Near Eastern Prophecy*, edited by Ehud Ben Zvi and Michael H. Floyd. Atlanta: Society of Biblical Literature, 2000.
Bennett, Gary M. "Oral Clarity in Preaching." DMin diss., Gordon-Conwell Theological Seminary, 2006.
Boadt, Lawrence. "The Poetry of Prophetic Persuasion: Preserving the Prophet's Persona." *The Catholic Biblical Quarterly* 59, no. 1 (1997) 1–21.
———. *Reading the Old Testament: An Introduction*. New York: Paulist Press, 1984.
Broadus, John A. *On the Preparation and Delivery of Sermons*, edited by J. B. Weatherspoon. New York: Harper & Row, 1944.

Bibliography

Brown, Francis, et al. *The New Brown, Driver, Briggs, Gesenius Hebrew and English Lexicon: With an Appendix Containing the Biblical Aramaic.* Peabody, Mass: Hendrickson, 1979.

Brueggemann, Walter. "The Book of Jeremiah: Portrait of the Prophet." *Interpretation* 37, no. 2 (April 1983) 130–45.

———. *An Introduction to the Old Testament: The Canon and Christian Imagination.* Louisville, KY: John Knox, 2012.

———. "Jeremiah's Use of Rhetorical Questions." *Journal of Biblical Literature* 92, no. 3 (1973) 358–74.

———. *The Prophetic Imagination.* Minneapolis, MN: Fortress, 1978.

———. *Reality, Grief, Hope: Three Urgent Prophetic Tasks.* Grand Rapids: Eerdmans, 2014.

Brueggemann, Walter, and Patrick D. Miller. *Like Fire in the Bones: Listening for the Prophetic Word in Jeremiah.* Minneapolis, MN: Fortress, 2006.

Bullock, C. Hassell. *An Introduction to the Old Testament Prophetic Books.* Chicago: Moody, 1986.

Caird, Gregory. *The Language and Imagery of the Bible.* Philadelphia: Westminster, 1980.

Calvin, John. *Ephesians.* Edinburgh: Banner of Truth, 1973.

Chapell, Bryan. *Christ-Centered Preaching: Redeeming the Expository Sermon.* Grand Rapids. Mich: Baker Academic, 2005.

Chisholm, Robert B. Jr. "'For Three Sins . . . Even for Four': The Numerical Sayings of Amos." *Bibliotheca Sacra* 147, no. 586 (1990) 188–97.

———. *Handbook on the Prophets.* Grand Rapids: Baker Academic, 2002.

———. "Structure, Style, and the Prophetic Message: An Analysis of Isaiah 5:8–30." *Bibliotheca Sacra* 143, no. 569 (1986) 46–60.

———. "Wordplay in the Eighth-Century Prophets." *Bibliotheca Sacra* 144, no. 573 (1987) 44–52.

Clendenen, E. Ray. "Textlinguistics and Prophecy in the Book of the Twelve." *Journal of the Evangelical Theological Society* 46, no. 3 (2003) 385–99.

Cook, Joan E. "Beyond 'Form Criticism and Beyond': James Muilenburg's Influence on a Generation of Biblical Scholars." *Proceedings* 17 (1997) 19–27.

Danker, Frederick W. *A Greek-English Lexicon of the New Testament and Other Early Christian Literature.* Third edition. Chicago: University of Chicago Press, 2000.

Davis, Ellen. *Swallowing the Scroll: Textuality and the Dynamic of Discourse in Ezekiel's Prophecy.* Sheffield: Almond, 1989.

Day, David. *Preaching with All You've Got: Embodying the Word.* Peabody, Mass: Hendrickson, 2006.

Devor, Richard C. "Whatever Happened to Prophetic Preaching." *Christian Ministry* 21, no. 4 (1990) 9–11.

Easley, Michael J. "Why Expository Preaching." In *The Moody Handbook of Preaching.* Ed. John M. Koessler and Michael J. Easley, 27–37. Chicago: Moody, 2008.

Edwards, O. C. *A History of Preaching.* Nashville: Abingdon, 2004.

Eswine, Zack. *Preaching to a Post-Everything World: Crafting Biblical Sermons That Connect with Our Culture.* Grand Rapids: Baker, 2008.

Evans, Craig A. *Jesus and the Ossuaries.* Waco, Texas: Baylor University Press, 2003.

Exley, Richard. "Overexposure: Transparent Preaching is not Without Risks." In *The Art and Craft of Biblical Preaching: A Comprehensive Resource for Today's Communicators*, edited by Haddon Robinson and Craig Brian Larson, 517–21. Grand Rapids: Zondervan, 2005.

BIBLIOGRAPHY

Farnell, F. David. "Is the Gift of Prophecy for Today: The Gift of Prophecy in the Old and New Testaments." *Bibliotheca Sacra* 149, no. 596 (1992) 387–410.

Fee, Gordon D. *God's Empowering Presence: The Holy Spirit in the Letters of Paul*. Peabody, MA: Hendrickson, 1994.

———. *Paul, the Spirit, and the People of God*. Peabody, MA: Hendrickson, 1996.

Feinberg, Charles Lee. *The Minor Prophets*. Chicago: Moody, 1976.

Forbes, James. *The Holy Spirit & Preaching*. Nashville: Abingdon, 1989.

Fox, Michael V. "The Rhetoric of Ezekiel's Vision of the Valley of the Bones." *Hebrew Union College Annual* 51 (1980) 1–15.

Furnish, Victor Paul. "Prophets, Apostles, and Preachers: a Study of the Biblical Concept of Preaching." *Interpretation* 17, no. 1 (1963) 48–60.

Garland, David E. *1 Corinthians*, Baker Exegetical Commentary on the New Testament. Grand Rapids: Baker Academic, 2008.

Gitay, Yehoshua. "Deutero-Isaiah: Oral or Written?" *Journal of Biblical Literature* 99, no. 2 (1980) 185–97.

———. "Prophetic Criticism—'What Are They Doing?': the Case of Isaiah—a Methodological Assessment." *Journal for the Study of the Old Testament* 96 (2001) 101–27.

———. "Reflections on the Study of the Prophetic Discourse." *Vetus Testamentum* XXXIII, 2 (1983) 207–21.

———. "Rhetorical Criticism and the Prophetic Discourse." In *Persuasive Artistry*, edited by Duane Frederick Watson, 13–24. Sheffield, England: JSOT Press, 1991.

———. "A Study of Amos's Art of Speech: A Rhetorical Analysis of Amos 3:1–15." *The Catholic Biblical Quarterly* 42, no. 3 (1980) 293–309.

Goldsworthy, Graeme. *Preaching the Whole Bible as Christian Scripture: The Application of Biblical Theology to Expository Preaching*. Grand Rapids: Eerdmans, 2000.

Gordon, Vic. "The New Testament in the New Millennium." In *Preaching to a Shifting Culture: 12 Perspectives on Communicating That Connects*, edited by Scott Gibson, 39–58. Grand Rapids: Baker, 2004.

Greidanus, Sidney. *The Modern Preacher and the Ancient Text: Interpreting and Preaching Biblical Literature*. Grand Rapids: Eerdmans, 1988.

———. *Preaching Christ from the Old Testament: A Contemporary Hermeneutical Method*. Grand Rapids: Eerdmans, 1999.

Grudem, Wayne A. *The Gift of Prophecy in the New Testament and Today*. Wheaton, IL: Crossway, 2000.

Guinness, Os. *Fool's Talk: Recovering the Art of Christian Persuasion*. Downers Grove: IVP, 2015.

Gunkel, Hermann. "The Israelite Prophecy from the Time of Amos." In *Twentieth Century Theology in the Making*, edited by Jaroslav Pelikan. Translated by R. A. Wilson, 48–75. New York: Harper & Row, 1970.

Hallo, William W. "Jonah and the Uses of Parody." In *Thus Says the Lord*, edited by John Ahn and Stephen Cook, 285–91. New York: T & T Clark, 2009.

Hans, Daniel T. "Preaching Through Personal Pain." In *The Art and Craft of Biblical Preaching: A Comprehensive Resource for Today's Communicators*, edited by Haddon Robinson and Craig Brian Larson, 95–98. Grand Rapids: Zondervan, 2005.

Harris, R. Laird, Gleason L. Archer, and Bruce K. Waltke. *Theological Wordbook of the Old Testament*, vol. 2. Chicago: Moody, 1980.

BIBLIOGRAPHY

Hauerwas, Stanley. "The Pastor as Prophet: Ethical Reflections on an Improbable Mission." In *Pastor as Prophet*, edited by Earl E. Shelp and Ronald H. Sunderland, 27–48. New York: Pilgrim, 1985.

Heisler, Greg. *Spirit-Led Preaching: The Holy Spirit's Role in Sermon Preparation and Delivery*. Nashville: B & H Academic, 2007.

Heschel, Abraham Joshua. *The Prophets*. New York: Harper & Row, 1962.

Hoehner, Harold W. *Ephesians: An Exegetical Commentary*. Grand Rapids: Baker Academic, 2002.

House, Paul R. *Lamentations*. Word Biblical Commentary 23B. Dallas: Word, 2004.

Howard, David M., Jr. "Rhetorical Criticism in Old Testament Studies." *Bulletin for Biblical Research* 4 (1994) 87–104.

Kennedy, George A. *Classical Rhetoric and Its Christian and Secular Tradition from Ancient to Modern Times*. Chapel Hill: University of North Carolina Press, 1980.

Kistemaker, Simon. *Exposition of the Epistle of James and the Epistles of John*. Grand Rapids: Baker, 1986.

———. *Exposition of the First Epistle to the Corinthians*. Grand Rapids: Baker, 1993.

———. *Exposition of Peter and Jude*. Grand Rapids: Baker, 1987.

Koehler, Ludwig, et al. *The Hebrew and Aramaic Lexicon of the Old Testament*. New York: Brill, 1999.

Koessler, John M. "Losing the Center." In *The Moody Handbook of Preaching*, edited by John M. Koessler and Michael J. Easley, 15–25. Chicago: Moody, 2008.

———. "View from the Pew: How to Hold the Attention of the Easily Distracted." In *The Art and Craft of Biblical Preaching: A Comprehensive Resource for Today's Communicators*, edited by Haddon Robinson and Craig Brian Larson, 124–26. Grand Rapids: Zondervan, 2005.

Kugel, James L. *The Idea of Biblical Poetry*. New Haven: Yale University Press, 1981.

Kuruvilla, Abraham. *Privilege the Text: A Theological Hermeneutic for Preaching*. Chicago: Moody, 2015.

Labuschagne, C. J. *The Incomparability of Yahweh in the Old Testament*. Leiden: Brill, 1966.

Lane, William L. *Hebrews 1–8*, Word Biblical Commentary 47A, Dallas: Word, 2002.

Larsen, David L. *The Company of the Preachers: A History of Biblical Preaching from the Old Testament to the Modern Era*. Grand Rapids: Kregel, 1998.

Leoh, Vincent. "A Pentecostal Preacher as an Empowered Witness." *Asian Journal of Pentecostal Studies* 9, no. 1 (2006) 35–58.

Lessing, R. Reed. "Orality in the Prophets." *Concordia Journal* 29, no. 2 (2003) 152–165.

———. "Preaching Like the Prophets: Using Rhetorical Criticism in the Appropriation of Old Testament Prophetic Literature." *Concordia Journal* 28, no. 4 (2002) 391–408.

Lessing, R. Reed, and Andrew E. Steinmann. *Prepare the Way of the Lord: An Introduction to the Old Testament*. Saint Louis: Concordia, 2014.

Levison, John R. "Did the Spirit Inspire Rhetoric? An Exploration of George Kennedy's Definition of Early Christian Rhetoric." In *Persuasive Artistry: Studies in New Testament Rhetoric in Honor of George A. Kennedy*, 25–40. Sheffield, England: Bloomsbury, 1991.

Liddell, H. G. *A Lexicon: Abridged from Liddell and Scott's Greek-English Lexicon*. Oak Harbor, WA: Logos Research Systems, 1996.

Lincoln, Andrew T. *Ephesians*, Word Biblical Commentary 42. Dallas: Word, 1990.

Long, D. Stephen. "Prophetic Preaching." In *Concise Encyclopedia of Preaching*, edited by W. H. Willimon and R. Lischer. Louisville: John Knox, 1995.

Lovell, George, and Neil Richardson. *Sustaining Preachers and Preaching: A Practical Guide*. London: T & T Clark, 2011.
Lundbom, Jack R. *The Hebrew Prophets: An Introduction*. Minneapolis: Fortress, 2010.
———. *Jeremiah: a Study in Ancient Hebrew Rhetoric*. Winona Lake, IN: Eisenbrauns, 1997.
Lybrand, Fred R. *Preaching on your Feet*. Nashville: Broadman & Holman, 2008.
MacArthur, John. *Preaching: How to Preach Biblically*. Nashville: Thomas Nelson, 1992.
MacDonald, Gordon. "Speaking into Crisis." In *The Art and Craft of Biblical Preaching: A Comprehensive Resource for Today's Communicators*, edited by Haddon Robinson and Craig Brian Larson, 641–45. Grand Rapids: Zondervan, 2005.
Mathewson, Steven D. "Outlines That Work for You, Not Against You: How to Write Sermon Points that Follow the Way People Think." In *The Art and Craft of Biblical Preaching: A Comprehensive Resource for Today's Communicators*, edited by Haddon Robinson and Craig Brian Larson, 360–63. Grand Rapids: Zondervan, 2005.
Matthews, Victor Harold. *The Hebrew Prophets and Their Social World: An Introduction*. Grand Rapids: Baker Academic, 2012.
McMickle, Marvin. *Where Have All the Prophets Gone? Reclaiming Prophetic Preaching in America*. Cleveland: The Pilgrim Press, 2006.
Merrill, Eugene H. *New American Commentary: Deuteronomy*, Vol. 4. Nashville: Broadman & Holman, 1994.
Meyer, F. B. *Expository Preaching Plans and Methods*. New York: Hodder & Stoughton, George H. Doran Co, 1912.
Miller, Kevin A. "Learning from the Giants." In *The Art & Craft of Biblical Preaching: A Comprehensive Resource for Today's Communicators*, edited by Haddon Robinson and Craig Brian Larson, 711–15. Grand Rapids: Zondervan, 2005.
Möller, Karl. *A Prophet in Debate: The Rhetoric of Persuasion in the Book of Amos*. New York: Sheffield Academic Press, 2003.
Moshavi, Adina. "What Can I Say? Implications and Communicative Functions of Rhetorical 'WH' Questions in Classical Biblical Hebrew Prose." *Vetus Testamentum*, 64, no. 1 (2014) 93–108.
Muilenburg, James. "Form Criticism and Beyond." *Journal of Biblical Literature* 88, no. 1 (1969) 1–18.
Neely, Winfred Omar. "Sermons That Move." In *The Moody Handbook of Preaching*, edited by John M. Koessler and Michael J. Easley, 323–34. Chicago: Moody, 2008.
Niditch, Susan. *Oral World and Written Word*. Louisville: John Knox, 1996.
Nissinen, Martti. "What is Prophecy? An Ancient Near Eastern Perspective." In *Inspired Speech: Prophecy in the Ancient Near East: Essays in Honor of Herbert B. Huffmon*, edited by John Kaltner and Louis Stulman, 17–37. London: T & T Clark, 2004.
O'Brien, Peter T. *The Letter to the Ephesians*. Grand Rapids: Eerdmans, 1999.
Oden, Thomas C. *Pastoral Theology: Essentials in Ministry*. San Francisco: Harper, 1983.
Overdorf, Daniel. *Applying the Sermon: How to Balance Biblical Integrity and Cultural Relevance*. Grand Rapids: Kregel, 2009.
Overstreet, R. Larry. *Persuasive Preaching: A Biblical and Practical Guide to the Effective Use of Persuasion*. Wooster, OH: Weaver, 2014.
Park, Sangyil. "Speaking of Hope: Prophetic Preaching." *Review and Expositor* 109 (2012) 413–27.
Parunak, H. van Dyke. "Oral Typesetting: Some Uses of Biblical Structure." *Biblica* 62, no. 2 (1981) 153–68.

Bibliography

———. "Some Axioms for Literary Architecture." *Semitics* 8 (1983) 1–16.
———. "Transitional Techniques in the Bible." *Journal of Biblical Literature* 102, no. 4 (1983) 525–48.
Perkins, William. *The Art of Prophesying; with, The Calling of the Ministry*. Edinburgh: Banner of Truth, 1996.
Pinker, Aron. "Historical Allusions in the Book of Habakkuk." *Jewish Biblical Quarterly* 36, no. 3 (2008) 143–52.
Quicke, Michael J. *360-Degree Preaching*. Grand Rapids: Baker Academic, 2003.
———. "History of Preaching: Assessing Today's Preaching in Light of History." In *The Art & Craft of Biblical Preaching: A Comprehensive Resource for Today's Communicators*, edited by Haddon Robinson and Craig Brian Larson, 64–69. Grand Rapids: Zondervan, 2005
Rad, Gerhard von. *The Message of the Prophets*. New York: Harper & Row, 1962.
———. *Old Testament Theology*, vol. 2, *The Theology of Israel's Prophetic Traditions*. Translated by D. M. G. Stalker. London: Oliver & Boyd, 1965.
Regt, L. J. de. "Discourse Implications of Rhetorical Questions in Job, Deuteronomy and the Minor Prophets." In *Literary Structure and Rhetorical Strategies in the Hebrew Bible*, edited by L. J. de Regt and Jan de Waard, 51–78. Assen, Netherlands: Eisenbrauns, 1996.
Richard, Ramesh. *Scripture Sculpture: A Do-It-Yourself Manual for Biblical Preaching*. Grand Rapids: Baker, 1995.
Robinson, Haddon W. *Biblical Preaching: The Development and Delivery of Expository Messages*. 2nd ed. Grand Rapids: Baker Academic, 2001.
———. "Blending Bible Content and Life Application." In *The Art and Craft of Biblical Preaching: A Comprehensive Resource for Today's Communicators*, edited by Haddon Robinson and Craig Brian Larson, 294–99. Grand Rapids: Zondervan, 2005.
———. "Clearly: How to Preach so Everyone Understands." In *The Art and Craft of Biblical Preaching: A Comprehensive Resource for Today's Communicators*, edited by Haddon Robinson and Craig Brian Larson, 333–35. Grand Rapids: Zondervan, 2005.
———. "Convictions of Biblical Preaching." In *The Art and Craft of Biblical Preaching: A Comprehensive Resource for Today's Communicators*, edited by Haddon Robinson and Craig Brian Larson, 23–24. Grand Rapids: Zondervan, 2005.
———. *Expository Preaching: Its Principles and Practice*. Leicester, UK: Inter-Varsity, 1986.
Robinson, Haddon W., and Scott M. Gibson, eds. *Making a Difference in Preaching: Haddon Robinson on Biblical Preaching*. Grand Rapids: Baker, 1999.
Sandnes, Karl Olav. *Paul, One of the Prophets?: A Contribution to the Apostle's Self-Understanding*. Trans. Paul Siebeck. Tübingen: J. C. B. Mohr, 1991.
Scharf, Greg and Bryan Chapell. *Let the Earth Hear His Voice: Strategies for Overcoming Bottlenecks in Preaching God's Word*. Phillipsburg: P&R, 2015.
Sensing, Timothy R. "A Call to Prophetic Preaching." *Restoration Quarterly* 41, no. 3 (January 1, 1999) 139–54.
Shelly, Rubel. *Written in Stone: Ethics for the Heart*. West Monroe, LA: Howard Publishing, 1994.
Smith, Gary V. *The Prophets as Preachers: An Introduction to the Hebrew Prophets*. Nashville, TN: Broadman & Holman, 1994.

Bibliography

Smith, Preserved, and Charles M. Jacobs, eds., *Luther's Correspondence and Other Contemporary Letters, Vol. II*. Philadelphia: United Lutheran Publishing House, 1918.

Smith, Ralph L. *Micah-Malachi*, Word Biblical Commentary vol. 32. Dallas: Word, 2002.

Spalding, George Hurley. "The Hebrew Prophet and the Christian Preacher." *Andover Review* 14, no. 81 (1890) 280–91.

Spurgeon, C. H. *Lectures to My Students, Complete & Unabridged*. Grand Rapids: Zondervan, 1954.

Stowell, Joe. "Self-Disclosure that Glorifies Christ." In *Art and Craft of Biblical Preaching: A Comprehensive Resource for Today's Communicators*, edited by Haddon Robinson and Craig Brian Larson, 143–44. Grand Rapids: Zondervan, 2005.

Stuart, Douglas. *Hosea-Jonah*, Vol. 31. Word Biblical Commentary. Dallas: Word, 2002.

Sunukjian, Donald. "Amos." In *The Bible Knowledge Commentary: An Exposition of the Scriptures by Dallas Seminary Faculty: Old Testament*, 1425–52. Wheaton, IL: Victor, 1985.

———. "The Credibility of the Preacher." *Bibliotheca Sacra* 139, no. 555 (July 1982) 255–66.

———. *Invitation to Biblical Preaching: Proclaiming Truth With Clarity and Relevance*. Grand Rapids: Kregel, 2007.

———. "The Preacher as Persuader." In *Walvoord, a Tribute: Doctrinal Essays in Honor of 30 Years of Academic Leadership*, edited by Donald K. Campbell and John E. Walvoord, 289–99. Chicago: Moody, 1982.

———. "Questions That Put Muscle on Bone: What to Ask When Developing and Idea." In *The Art and Craft of Biblical Preaching: A Comprehensive Resource for Today's Communicators*, edited by Haddon Robinson and Craig Brian Larson, 338–52. Grand Rapids: Zondervan, 2005.

Thomas, Robert L. "Prophecy Rediscovered: A Review of the Gift of Prophecy in the New Testament and Today." *Bibliotheca Sacra* 149, no. 593 (1992) 83–96.

Thompson, Michael E. W. "Prayer, Oracle and Theophany: The Book of Habakkuk." *Tyndale Bulletin* 44:1 (1993) 33–53.

Tisdale, Leonora Tubbs. *Prophetic Preaching: A Pastoral Approach*. Louisville, KY: John Knox, 2010.

Veerman, David. "Apply Within: A Method for Finding the Practical Response Called for in a Text." In *The Art and Craft of Biblical Preaching: A Comprehensive Resource for Today's Communicators*, edited by Haddon Robinson and Craig Brian Larson, 283–88. Grand Rapids: Zondervan, 2005.

Wallace, Daniel B. *Greek Grammar Beyond the Basics: An Exegetical Syntax of the New Testament*. Grand Rapids: Zondervan, 1996.

Watts, John D. W. *Isaiah 1–33*, Word Biblical Commentary 24. Dallas: Word, 2002.

Whitney, Donald S. *Praying the Bible*. Wheaton, IL: Crossway, 2015.

Wiersbe, Warren. *Preaching and Teaching with Imagination: the Quest for Biblical Ministry*. Wheaton, IL: Victor, 1994.

Willhite, Keith. "Connecting with Your Congregation." In *Preaching to a Shifting Culture: 12 Perspectives on Communicating that Connects*, edited by Scott Gibson, 95–111. Grand Rapids: Baker, 2004.

———. *Preaching with Relevance: Without Dumbing Down*. Grand Rapids: Kregel, 2001.

BIBLIOGRAPHY

Willimon, William H. "'Would That All the Lord's People Were Prophets': Pentecost Preaching as Prophetic Preaching: Texts for Prophets." *Journal For Preachers* 16, no. 4 (1993) 16–21.

Wilson, Robert R. "Current Issues in the Study of Old Testament prophecy." In *Inspired Speech: Prophecy in the Ancient Near East : Essays in Honor of Herbert B. Huffmon*, edited by John Kaltner and Louis Stulman, 38–45. London: T & T Clark, 2004.

———. *Prophecy and Society in Ancient Israel*. Philadelphia, Pa: Fortress, 2011.

Worral, Kelli. "Drama and the Sermon." In *The Moody Handbook of Preaching*, edited by John M. Koessler and Michael J. Easley, 293–307. Chicago: Moody, 2008.

Wuellner, Wilhelm H. "Where is Rhetorical Criticism Taking Us." *Catholic Biblical Quarterly* 49, no. 3 (1987) 448–63.

Zuck, Roy "The Role of The Holy Spirit in Christian Teaching." In *The Christian Educator's Handbook on Teaching*, edited by Kenneth O. Gangel and Howard G. Hendricks, 32–44. Wheaton, IL: Victor, 1988.

Scripture Index

GENESIS

8:21	68
22	139
41:28, 38	41

EXODUS

3:12	116
7:1–2	16
31:3	47
34:7	32
35:31	47

LEVITICUS

26:4	76
27	139

NUMBERS

6:22–27	63
11:25–29	41
24:2–4	41

DEUTERONOMY

7:6–8	30
13:1–5	16, 21
18:15–18	3n4
18:15–22	16
18:16–17	17
18:20–22	43n7
28	18n20
28:12	76
30:1–6	33

1 SAMUEL

10:10	41
17:34	121
19:23	41
22:1	82, 144–45

2 SAMUEL

1:19–20	82
12:1–15	61, 111
17:1–14	73
22:34	144
23:2	41

Scripture Index

1 KINGS

18:27–29	42
22:8–18	93

2 KINGS

16:7	123
17:13	17

2 CHRONICLES

15:1	41
18:23	41
20:14	41

JOB

32:18–20	144

PSALMS

2:4, 11, 12	56
11:5	144
16:6	127–28
22:7	144
39:2–3	144
62:8	147
69:33	144
78:1, 4	69
78:40–58	55
95	43

PROVERBS

30:15–31	62

ECCLESIASTES

12:10–11	70

ISAIAH

1:7–8	67
1:18	31, 73
5:1–7	103
5:1–30	76–81, 77n23
5:4–5	98–99
5:8–23	106
2:1–3	18
6:5	79n29, 129
6:9	141
6:9–10	141n3
6:9–13	77, 80
7:1–17	141
7:1–25	74, 123
7:14	31, 33
9:1–6	33
9:6	31
13–21	21
20:1–6	135
20:2	135n18
20:3	7
31:4	121
40–66	33
40:1–11	83
41:21	72
43:26	72
51:9–11	31
53	31
53:10	123
54:1	27
55:1	28
56:10	28
57:3	28
61:1–2	50
61:1–11	50
63–65	31
63:7–10	55
65:2	142
65:13	141

JEREMIAH

1:1–19	94
1:6	129
2:1–9	30, 31

2:1—3:5	94–98, 100–101, 102–3
2:14	87
2:19	102n21
2:31–32	87
3:1–5	87
5:13	42
7:21–26	31
7:27	142
8:4	87
8:19, 22	88
9:1	142
11:1–5	31
11:1–8	29
11:4, 7	30
13:1–11	135
14:1–6	122
16:1–9	131
16:14–15	35
18:14–15	87
19:1–13	135
20:1–2	142
20:7–9	142–44
20:7–10	148
20:11–13	143, 148
20:14–18	148
23:5–6	33
23:7–8	35
26:1–11	93
27:1—29:10	123–25
31:31–33	35
31:31–34	51
31:31–37	33
32:1–15	132
32:1–44	33, 132
32:17–23	31
33:19–20	123
34:13–16	31
35:1–19	136
36:2	109n39
37:11–20	142
38:1–9	142
46–51	21

LAMENTATIONS

3:22–24	144
3:47 (48)	83

EZEKIEL

2:3–7	145
2:7	141
3:16–21	146
3:22–27	137
4:1–3	137
4:9–17	137
5:1–12	137
8:1–18	34
12:1–20	137
15:1–8	120
16:1–63	120
20:5–7	31
21:1–32	137
25—32	21
26:3–21	104–6
33:2–9	146
36:26–27	51
37:1–28	34, 120–21
37:15–28	137
37:3	88
40–47	33

DANIEL

1:8	30, 147
2:17–22	147
3:18–19	30
6:3–15	147
9:2	144
9:4–15	147
9:15	31
9:20–27	147

HOSEA

1:2—3:5	130–31, 135
1:2–3	146
1:2–9	67
1:10–11	34
3:1	34
4–9	67
4:6	32
9:7	42
11:1	32
11:8–9	131

JOEL

1:4	67
2:2	67
2:28	34
2:28–29	50
3:16–17	34

AMOS

1–2	61–64, 66, 87n40, 104
1:1	86
2:7–10	32
3–4	83–87
3:1–2	32
3:7	15
3:8	63
5:19	63
7:1–13	93
7:7–11	124–25
7:10–13	146
7:14	129
9:11, 14	34

OBADIAH

3–4	116
20–21	34

JONAH

1:1–2	16n16

MICAH

1:8	7
1:10–15	81–83
2:11	42
3:8	41
4:1–7	34
5:2–4	34
6:1–5	32
6:8	29
7:7	34
7:18–19	32

NAHUM

2:10	83

HABAKKUK

1:1–11	98
1:2	129
1:2–4	68
1:12—2:1	148
1:12—2:20	98
2:4	68
2:20	34
3:1–19	98, 123, 144–45
3:2	32, 68
3:3–19	32, 68
3:18	146

ZEPHANIAH

1:2	68
1:2—2:3	126
2:13—3:5	64n20
3:15	34

Scripture Index

HAGGAI

1:2–4	67
1:2, 8	116
1:12–14	141
1:12–15	116–17
1:13	41
2:1–9	117
2:5–6	32
2:7	34
2:11–14	118
2:15–19	119–20

ZECHARIAH

12–14	34

MALACHI

1–4	116
1:2, 6	99
1:10	68
2:11–16	125
2:13, 17	99
3:7, 13	99
3:7–12	126
3:16—4:6	101
3:17	34
4:4–6	34

MATTHEW

1:23	31
12:1–2	113
19:6	65
24:38	131

MARK

14:1–11	135–36

LUKE

1:3	53
1:15–17	44
1:41–43	44
1:67	44
2:11	31
4:18–19	50
16:31	48
24:46–49	43

JOHN

11:39	121
12:38	31
16:13	52
17:14–19	148

ACTS

1:8	44
2:4	44
2:4–36	47
2:11	44
2:14–40	44
2:17–21	36n20
2:38–40	36n20
2:42	3
3:13–26	36
4:8	47
4:8–12	44
4:29–31	45, 51
6:4	70
6:5	149
7:51	43
9:10–17	45
13:9	45, 47
13:17	36n20
13:34	36n20
13:47–52	45
17:6	28, 114
18:4	72
20:28, 34–35	36n20
28:25	43

Scripture Index

ROMANS

1:18—2:1	64
6:1–4	139
8:29–39	36
10:21	142
12:1	35
12:12	142

1 CORINTHIANS

1:21–22	50
2:1–5	71
2:2	36
2:4	51, 71
2:4–5	48
2:10–11	54
2:10–13	52
2:12–14	48
2:13	71
3:6	48
5:7–8	36
7:25–28	132
9:16	143
10:1	113
11:23–26	139
14:24–25	1, 2, 117
14:36–40	3

2 CORINTHIANS

3:3	52, 130
3:5–6	52
3:6	v
3:18	52
4:1–7	52
4:5	128–29
5:11	72
5:20	72
12:6	42
12:12	51

GALATIANS

6:17	128

EPHESIANS

1:7	36
1:11–14	36
1:23	47
2:1–10	36
3:19	47
3:20	3
4:1	36
4:10–16	47
4:11–13	47
4:24	55
4:25–32	55
4:30	55
5:18	45, 46, 47, 54
5:19	55
5:19–21	46
5:22	46n14
5:25	65
6:18–19	51

PHILIPPIANS

4:9	127, 139

COLOSSIANS

1:28–29	69, 138
4:2	146
4:3–4	92

1 THESSALONIANS

1:3, 9–10	37
1:5	49, 51
2:8	134
2:19	37
3:13	37
3:15	103

4:16–18	37
5:20–21	3
5:23	37

1 TIMOTHY

4:12–15	134

2 TIMOTHY

3:5	6
3:10–11	128
3:16	19, 39
4:2	19
4:2–4	140–41

TITUS

1:9	20
2:1–10	36
2:11–14	36
2:15	26, 37
2:15	3

HEBREWS

3:7	43
10:15	43
12:4	143

JAMES

5:10	140
5:17	133, 142

1 PETER

1:10–12	114
1:12	49
1:21	20, 74
1:24–25	31
2:5	117

2 PETER

1:21	43

1 JOHN

1:3–10	55
2:20, 27	50

JUDE

3	20

REVELATION

1:6	v

www.ingramcontent.com/pod-product-compliance
Lightning Source LLC
Chambersburg PA
CBHW050815160426
43192CB00010B/1772